The

LEADERSHIP
CONNECTION

The Link Between Leading and Succeeding

ERIK THERWANGER

The
LEADERSHIP
CONNECTION

The Link Between Leading and Succeeding

The Think **GREAT**®
COLLECTION

BALBOA.
PRESS
A DIVISION OF HAY HOUSE

Balboa Press books may be ordered through booksellers or by contacting:

Balboa Press
A Division of Hay House
1663 Liberty Drive
Bloomington, IN 47403
www.balboapress.com
1 (877) 407-4847

Print information available on the last page.

ISBN: 978-1-9822-1266-7 (sc)
ISBN: 978-1-9822-1268-1 (hc)
ISBN: 978-1-9822-1267-4 (e)

Library of Congress Control Number: 2018911927

Balboa Press rev. date: 03/30/2019

Dedication

This book is dedicated to the United States Marine Corps: the single greatest example of leadership I have ever experienced in my life. And to the Marines I have been blessed to train with, to follow, and to lead. Your commitment to making the Leadership Connection will always be the hallmark of my personal and professional life.

Semper Fi'

To every client I have worked with who has made the personal commitment to do more than fill a position of leadership. Your desire to fulfill your elite purposes of a leader, and impact the people you encounter, inspires me to become a greater leader on my own journey – my leadership expedition.

Lead with Purpose

Contents

3

PILLARS OF BUSINESS

GREATNESS

LEADING

PLANNING

SELLING

ThinkGREAT

The 3 Pillars

Supporting Your Growth

Build - Strengthen - Expand

No matter what industry you are in, your organization is supported by three distinct disciplines – leadership development, strategic planning, and sales performance. A structural break, in any single pillar, can significantly impact your ability to fulfill your mission and achieve your vision.

The 3 Pillars of Business Greatness provide you with the resources to unify all three, increasing their strength and providing the support and structure necessary to exceed your goals. Unique to the business world, these three essential programs will unify your people, with a shared dialogue, and create the greatest levels of structure, synergy, and success.

Developing your leaders, creating your strategic plan, and enhancing your sales system should not be taken lightly. Each book, *The LEADERSHIP Connection*, *ELEVATE*, and *Dynamic Sales COMBUSTION* forms a collective cohesion of strategies and techniques for greater results.

Welcome to Pillar 1... Leading!

The LEADERSHIP Connection will introduce you and your team to a new way of leading; one that focuses on achieving the highest levels of engagement in your people, while increasing the empowerment of your entire leadership team.

It's time to begin your own unique journey and realize your true leadership potential. By encouraging your team to step on the path with you, you will enhance your organization as you guide your team to new levels of success and achievement!

Introduction

Make the Decision to Lead

Your Position Does Not Make You a Leader – Your Choices Do.

The *art* of leading people has been studied throughout history. But in today's fast-paced environment, most leaders are thrust into leadership positions with little to no training on how to effectively lead others. Countless theories exist, thousands of books have been written, and people pay top-dollar to learn highly valued leadership skills at seminars. In fact, businesses invest hundreds of millions of dollars to train their teams to become better leaders. Why so much focus on leadership? It's simple; success is directly linked to leading.

With the click of a mouse, you can find virtually every available resource on this life-changing topic. When I first wrote this book in 2014, I typed *leadership* into Google and received 409,000,000 results. Today, in 2019, I performed the same search and received 4,510,000,000, Yes, over 4 billion! That's a lot of information to sift through. Perhaps you are looking to order some leadership materials like: books, videos, or audio resources. Let's look at Amazon and see what resources you can find. Click … 60,000 leadership results!

Leadership is a huge topic; one that can be a bit overwhelming and perhaps intimidating. It is often misunderstood, underutilized, and ineffectively implemented. But it is also the single most important factor to your success, the success of your team, and ultimately, the success of your organization. There is no doubt that improving your leadership skills, and the leadership skills of those on your team, will help you to achieve greater results. But where do you start?

Effectively leading your team will make the difference between winning and losing, between succeeding and failing. Every organization can benefit from this common denominator. Unfortunately, most fail to allocate the time and resources needed to develop the leaders on their teams. Yet the cost of building leadership, strengthening Pillar 1, is miniscule compared to the value it brings.

When I launched my company, Think GREAT, I had a simple goal: to translate my personal experiences into meaningful books and powerful presentations that would help people to achieve greater results in their lives. Since then, I authored six books, including *The GOAL Formula, Dynamic Sales Combustion, ELEVATE, The SCALE Factor,* and *GPS: Goal Planning Strategy.* I also became a professional speaker, and have been hired to train individuals, teams, and organizations on the concepts in these books.

As a corporate coach, I enjoy helping businesses to create a plan for their goals (*ELEVATE – Pillar 2*) and enhance their sales performance (*Dynamic Sales Combustion – Pillar 3*). I also help people to improve their health and fitness (*The SCALE Factor*). But the topic I am most requested to teach is... you guessed it, leadership (*The LEADERSHIP Connection – Pillar 1*).

I have had the privilege of working with thousands of team members, sales professionals, executives, and business owners. My presentations have been requested from companies such as U.S. Bank, charities including the American Cancer Society, and branches of the armed services like the United States Marine Corps – three vastly different organizations.

US Bank is a Fortune 500 company, The American Cancer Society is one of the largest cancer-fundraisers in the world, and the United States Marine Corps considers itself the most elite fighting force in the world. Although these three entities serve tremendously different purposes, they all share a common objective. Each organization wants to achieve greater results; they want to succeed. And to do that, they focus on developing their leaders.

As most people quickly discover, merely assuming a leadership position does not guarantee you will become an effective leader. As leaders, we have many roles. We are morale boosters, problem solvers, goal setters, and strategic planners. We are counselors, therapists, coaches, and cheerleaders all rolled into one. We organize meetings, resolve conflicts, and attempt to keep everyone productive (and happy). In addition to those duties, we still have our own job descriptions to fulfill. Keeping all of those "leadership" plates spinning can be a heavy burden, and that is without facing any personal challenges.

Another thing to consider is that you are typically responsible for continued growth within your team, department, and your entire organization. Leadership is not easy, but it is simple. The good news is that most leaders are fully capable of accomplishing all that is expected of them, and more. The bad news is that they lack the strategies, techniques, and shared-language necessary for making the link between leading and succeeding.

This is my specialty. I help leaders, and the members of their teams, to exceed their potential by making *The LEADERSHIP Connection*. Although I have always embraced my role as a leader, in every position I have held, there was a starting point for my leadership journey. Three weeks after turning eighteen, I experienced a defining moment that forever changed my perception of what it means to be a true leader.

MY FIRST FULL-TIME JOB

It was the summer of 1987, and I just graduated from high school. I had been working some part-time, under-the-table jobs, to earn a little cash. Cleaning buses, mowing lawns, and doing small projects provided me some spending money, but I was ready to do something greater with my life. I had made the decision to head in a new direction and was about to start my first full-time job. As you can imagine, I was a little nervous.

On August 24, 1987, my name became Recruit Therwanger as I exited the bus and entered the onboarding program for the United States Marine Corps – Boot Camp. Over the next ninety days, the young men in Platoon 1095 would be transformed from undisciplined civilians into hard-charging Marines.

Our transformation into "The Few and The Proud" did not occur by stepping into camouflage uniforms, shaving our heads, or doing countless push-ups. We did all of that and much more. We quickly learned that becoming a Marine was about becoming a leader. For the next three months, our platoon would be in the constant presence of dedicated, passionate, and very loud Marine Corps drill instructors (DI's) – our on-boarders.

Our four DI's were intense, laser-focused, and fully committed to ensuring that we accomplished our goal: earning the title of U.S. Marine. They embodied the essence of leadership and taught us the traits and principles that were expected of all Marines. Graduating from boot camp and becoming a Marine was not merely the end of my basic training, it was the beginning of my life-long leadership journey – my personal expedition as a leader.

In 1991, as the First Gulf War ended, so did my tour of duty. I was honorably discharged from the Marine Corps. Corporal Therwanger became Erik again. Although I might have packed away my uniforms, I would forever keep with me the leadership skills I developed as a Marine. I had been surrounded by an uplifting leadership culture; one that guided my actions, helped me to overcome obstacles, and was my support system during four years of service.

Now it was time to apply what I had learned to my new life. But the level of leadership I had grown accustomed to was hard to find in the civilian sector. Gone was the intense focus of my drill instructors, the unique perspectives of my Staff Non-Commissioned Officers (NCOs), and the direct guidance of my officers.

Because my goals and dreams were of the utmost importance, I made the choice to apply the leadership skills I had learned in the Marine Corps to every facet of my new direction in life. I made the decision to lead, and it helped me to stay the course as I pursued all of my goals. Whether I was studying in a university classroom or making a presentation in an executive board room, my leadership development gave me unbreakable strength.

In business, a lack of leadership can cost money. But in combat, it can cost lives. Although I have spent far more time in a suit and tie than I have in a camouflage uniform, the leadership development I received from the Marine Corps has provided me an unparalleled edge in the business world. Now, you can use that edge to gain distinct advantages in your career and in your life.

MAKING THE LEADERSHIP CONNECTION

Most leaders want to experience the benefits of leadership but struggle to properly implement it into their organizations. As a trainer, I work closely with all levels of leaders. I coach those who are new to leadership, and I mentor experienced leaders. I train supervisors, managers, executives, military commanders, and business owners.

You would likely agree that each position in your organization should serve a specific purpose. Typically, team members who fulfill those positions help an organization to *survive*. They complete the tasks needed to ensure that the organization moves forward.

But more importantly, I believe each leadership position serves elite purposes. A leader should help an organization to *thrive* and to accomplish the goals necessary to ensure that everyone moves forward. Regardless of their position, most leaders struggle because they do not understand how to link together their purposes.

The LEADERSHIP Connection will help your organization to succeed by explaining how to successfully link together:

The Four Elite Purposes (EPs) of a Leader:

1. **E**nhance **P**erceptions

2. **E**levate **P**riorities

3. **E**mpower **P**eople

4. **E**xceed **P**ossibilities

If you are ready to experience new levels of success, then it is time to take the steps to make leadership the foundation in your organization. Imagine how it will feel as you make this connection in your company. Imagine what your results would be like as you and your team begin to make *The LEADERSHIP Connection.*

Earlier, when I mentioned that leadership was a huge topic, I asked the question, "Where do you start?" Your leadership journey does not begin when you are appointed to your position. It begins when you make the decision to lead. *The LEADERSHIP Connection* is much more than just a starting point. It will be your guide as you embark on your own unique leadership expedition and commit to making the link between leading and succeeding.

This book is the culmination of my unique experiences as a leader, spanning nearly three decades. I have had the opportunity to flex my leadership muscles as a shift supervisor, a facility manager, a branch office manager, and as an executive business leader. It is the leadership principles in this book that allowed me to rise from an entry-level job to vice president, while working at a post-production company in the entertainment industry.

I earned the title of VP in less than eighteen months from the day I was hired because my primary focus was leading. I developed the leaders around me, launched a dedicated and focused sales team, and helped to create a corporate culture that allowed for many areas of success, including the growth of our annual revenue by over 300 percent. But that journey all began with leadership.

As you make *The LEADERSHIP Connection*, you will discover that the benefits of leadership do not end at your office door. They positively transform your entire life and magnify your results. In addition to all of the professional growth you will experience, you will also find your personal life will be forever enriched.

The LEADERSHIP Connection will be your personal guide to developing your leadership skills and transforming your organization into a cohesive team of leaders, capable of accomplishing all objectives. Starting today, the choice is yours to make *The LEADERSHIP Connection*!

Think GREAT,

Erik

Expedition Assessment

The Elite Leadership System (ELS)

Continuous effort, not strength or intelligence, is the key to unlocking our potential.

~ Winston Churchill

Expedition Assessment

The Elite Leadership System (ELS)

Inspecting Your Leadership Capabilities.

If you were accused of being a leader, would there be enough evidence to convict you? Would they throw the book at you or let you off with a warning – a light slap on the wrist? Unfortunately, most people who are in leadership positions would never be found guilty of being a leader. They not only lack the dialogue, the shared language of leadership, but they rarely inspect their leadership actions and corresponding results.

During my four years in the Marine Corps, I consistently participated in inspections. Each week, our barracks was inspected, sometimes with a white glove, to ensure that we maintained a squared-away living environment. Yes, that's a tough one to pass!

We were required to pass uniform inspections, guaranteeing that we possessed all of the required gear. Our rifles were checked, our physical abilities were reviewed, and our gas masks were assessed. Even our work environments were regularly inspected. In fact, each week, we performed a "Field Day" – a detailed cleaning of our entire work area.

Inspections are critical for sustainable success because they establish high expectations and require guidelines for achieving them. Inspections create a mindset within your team - the perception that they can achieve the highest levels of excellence. Imagine the possibilities if we had an inspection to assess the "leadership" performance of our leaders and ourselves.

If you plan on buying a home, home inspections are a must. This visual analysis provides a detailed look at the current condition of the property you want to purchase. Without this inspection, you may not find the hidden mold or the unwelcome termites. Foregoing a home inspection could result in significant and costly repairs. Without a leadership inspection, you, too, could face significant and costly repairs. Vehicles are also inspected to ensure they operate properly. Before embarking on a road trip, it makes sense to inspect the performance of your car – check the tires, check the lights, check the fluid levels. Before aircraft fly into the heavens, they are intensely inspected. Even trains are under constant review before leaving the station.

I suppose it is critical to inspect vehicles, if we expect them to go somewhere. Perhaps the same thought process should apply to leaders, if we want them to go somewhere. It is detrimental to an organization when a leader remains motionless. I have found that most businesses fail to inspect the performance of their leaders, until something goes wrong.

Businesses routinely use quality control inspections to guarantee the dependability of their products and the efficiencies of their systems. Many use their QC process as a powerful marketing tool to build consumer confidence. There are many benefits of providing inspections in the workplace.

The Benefits of Inspections:

- Detects problems before they escalate into costly issues
- Increases team awareness of processes/systems
- Encourages greater attention-to-detail
- Elevates satisfaction
- Increases effective utilization of resources
- Strengthens the bottom-line
- Positively impacts culture
- Improves team morale/pride
- Increases sales
- Enhances best practices

It's fair to say that these benefits would also apply to leaders, not just to products. It's easy to see the value of inspecting our products and processes but also easy to neglect the assessment of our leaders.

THE ELITE LEADERSHIP SYSTEM - ELS

The power of inspections cannot be denied and should never be overlooked. But most businesses do not have a system for gauging the capabilities of their leaders; discovering how effective their leadership skills are. Your people are far too valuable to allow leaders to only fill a position when they could fulfill a purpose.

Just as a simple seed can grow into a powerful and unwavering tree, The *Elite Leadership System* will allow you to grow, teach, and cultivate your leaders as you foster an environment of leadership development by making *The LEADERSHIP Connection* and implementing the four steps for growing leaders.

The Four-Step for Growing Plants:

1. Select Seeds

2. Choose a location to plant

3. Sow (Plant) your seeds

4. Cultivate (Nurture)

The Four-Steps for Growing Elite Leaders (Elite Purposes):

1. Enhance Perceptions

2. Elevate Priorities

3. Empower People

4. Exceed Possibilities

OUR GUIDE FOR TRANSFORMING LEADERS

The LEADERSHIP Connection is your handbook, designed for you to share with your entire team, planting the leadership seeds that will grow your people – at all levels. This leadership inspection tool is divided into four powerful sections and will guide you, step-by-step, to define and enhance each component of a highly effective leadership team.

Part I: Enhance Perceptions

Your people will see things differently as you *Clearly Define Leadership* and provide a solid understanding of the role of leaders in your organization. As you *Develop a Unifying Culture* you will increase the identity of your team, positioning them to *Identify Priority Goals* and strive to accomplish them.

Part II: Elevate Priorities

Everyone feels busy, but the key to success is leading a productive team. You and your people will be issued a "leadership" bar and will understand how to *Raise Expectations* together. Instead of dumping tasks on one another, each leader will discover how to *Delegate with a Purpose* and *Increase Accountability*, so everyone will stay on course.

Part III: Empower People

Empowering people is critically important, and your team will learn how to dynamically deliver messages as they enhance their *Communication* skills. Providing more than training, you will begin to develop your people as you master *Cultivation*, which leads to the creation of an environment that produces innovative solutions through *Collaboration.*

Part IV: Exceed Possibilities

Just as every building began with blueprints, you and your team will *Have a Plan* for high levels of success. You will learn how to *Build Leaders* around you to support the goals in your plan. While striving to *Become a Visionary Leader*, you will encourage your team to courageously step into the future and accomplish more than they ever thought possible.

I began to develop the concept of *The LEADERSHIP Connection* once I entered the civilian workforce in 1991. Leaving the Marine Corps, it became blatantly obvious that true leadership development was nearly non-existent in most organizations. Although many people were in leadership positions, most of them rarely performed like leaders and the impact on their teams was severe.

As the vice president of the media company, I remember when two of our larger competitors closed their facilities in Santa Monica. Why did their clients leave them and come to us? Did we have better equipment? No! Did we have better materials (video tapes, DVDs, etc.)? No! Did we have a better facility? No!

Undeniably, we had better people; our team had been developed to think and act like leaders. Hands down, our 300% growth was a result of developing leaders at every level, from our owner to our drivers, and everyone in between. We did not manage our way to success, we led our way there. Provide your teams with more than just job training; provide leadership development.

The LEADERSHIP Connection is not a collection of leadership theories that may work. This book is the culmination of proven strategies and techniques that I now share with business leaders across the country to transform their leaders, their cultures, and their results.

Throughout the pages of *The LEADERSHIP Connection,* you will encounter powerful ideas to make greater connections; a *Leadership Link,* just like the one below. These tips, concepts, and insights will further enhance your leadership journey with your team.

Leadership Link Invest time to inspect your leaders, not just to inspect your products and processes.

90 DAYS

You will discover that the books in my series, *The Think GREAT Collection,* share a common theme regarding time. I fully believe in the transformational power of 90 days. I have used 90-Day Flight Plans to elevate business results through strategic planning, harnessed the power of 90-Day Races to increase sales activities, and I personally use 90-Day Runs to accomplish important short-term personal goals.

Within 90 days, I transformed from a civilian to a United States Marine. Imagine the possibilities for you and your leadership team in the next 90 days. Imagine when you connect 90-day blocks of time together and consistently assess your performance as leaders.

EXPEDITION ASSESSMENT

If you were to embark on a long hiking expedition, let's say for the next 90 days, you would have a lot to think about. For starters, you must consider the weather, terrain, altitude, and environment where you will be hiking. But that's not all.

Before taking your first step, it would make sense to assess the gear you are taking. You not only want to have the right equipment, but you want to make sure that everything works correctly. Some of the most important items to remember:

- ☐ Backpack
- ☐ Water
- ☐ Food
- ☐ Cell Phone

- ☐ First Aid Kit
- ☐ Lighter/Matches
- ☐ Utensils
- ☐ Shelter

As you embark on your leadership journey, regular assessments of your leadership capabilities will not only allow you to identify where you are, but it will show you where you need to grow. Assessments build confidence and allow leaders to understand the expectations of leadership.

You and your team will be more effective and efficient when leading your people by completing your *Leadership Performance Checklist* (next page), a 12-point assessment to check the capabilities of your leaders. Enhancing a leadership skill is more effective than continually replacing leaders because they were never developed. Let's take an assessment of leadership skills before your journey begins.

LEADERSHIP
Performance Checklist

Gauge the status of your leaders before attempting to march forward. Rank each, on a scale of 1-10, 10 being best.

Leadership definition understood	1	2	3	4	5	6	7	8	9	10
Our culture unifies our people	1	2	3	4	5	6	7	8	9	10
Priority goals are established	1	2	3	4	5	6	7	8	9	10
High expectations are set	1	2	3	4	5	6	7	8	9	10
Delegation occurs and empowers	1	2	3	4	5	6	7	8	9	10
We achieve voluntary accountability	1	2	3	4	5	6	7	8	9	10
We dynamically communicate	1	2	3	4	5	6	7	8	9	10
We cultivate our people	1	2	3	4	5	6	7	8	9	10
Our people collaborate/innovate	1	2	3	4	5	6	7	8	9	10
We have and use a strategic plan	1	2	3	4	5	6	7	8	9	10
We consistently build leaders	1	2	3	4	5	6	7	8	9	10
Our vision is understood and shared	1	2	3	4	5	6	7	8	9	10

Part I

Enhance Perceptions

Part I

Enhance Perceptions

Is Your Leadership Glass Half Empty or Half Full?

Have you ever made an exciting announcement to your team and their response was less than enthusiastic? If so, you are not alone. Leaders often roll out dynamic enhancements, inspiring plans, and motivational messages to their teams, only to be met with the resounding sound of... silence. What went wrong? You were excited. They should be excited too, right?

For a brief moment you think it might be your delivery, or even your timing. But deep inside, you know it was something else. Ultimately, what you *perceived* to be amazing was not *seen* the same way by your audience. When the perceptions of your team fail to align with your own vision, the outcome of such a mismatch can have a devastating impact on your desired results.

Leaders are often left feeling discouraged, frustrated, and sometimes a bit angered by the lack of enthusiasm from their team members. On the other hand, team members are often unimpressed, negative, and sometimes a bit disappointed by the message they receive from their leaders. A definitive "connection" failed to be made by the leader.

It is not uncommon for leaders to say to me, "I wish we were all on the same page." When the perceptions of the team and the leaders are not connected, or worse yet, the perceptions of the leadership team are not aligned, you cannot expect to reach the full potential of your organization. Perhaps you are thinking, "Enhancing someone's perception can be a challenging task." Welcome to leadership. Here is some GREAT news... the ball is in your court! You possess the ability to significantly enhance the perceptions of your team.

Every team member views things differently: policies and procedures, their job duties, the responsibilities of others, workflow, management, the organization's goals, the challenges facing them, and even the contents of what needs to be in the vending machine, just to name a few. The list could go on and on. But no matter how long the list is, their perceptions will affect the way they see you as a leader and how they work toward your organization's common goals.

The ability to understand your team's mindset is challenging enough. But as a leader, you must strive to enhance their perceptions in order to unify your team and position your organization for success. Even though people might see the same thing, they can perceive it differently, and there is a huge difference between these two words.

Seeing: the physical ability for our brains to translate the data that enters our eyes and transform it into "images" so we can **interpret our environment**.

Perceiving: the mental ability for our brains to translate the data that enters our minds and transform it into "meaning" so we can **interpret our circumstances**.

As a leader, the environment you help to create in your organization is critical for your team to perform their duties. But your ability to connect with them and enhance their perceptions will allow them to conquer their circumstances, paving the way for continued growth and success. As a leader, that is what you are striving for, isn't it? Continued growth and success?

THE IMPORTANCE OF PERCEPTIONS

We are all familiar with the cliché, "Perception is reality." If we, as leaders, do not focus on enhancing the perceptions of our team, the reality could be disastrous. So, let's take a closer look at how *perception* is defined and how we can move ourselves and our team members to fostering the perception of being a leader.

perception

noun

- The act or faculty of apprehending by means of the senses or of the mind; cognition; **understanding**.

- The way you think about or **understand** someone or something.

- The ability to **understand** or notice something easily.

- The way that you notice or **understand** something using one of your senses.

It is evident from these definitions that our perceptions are how we understand things: people, situations, processes, and every form of communication. It is also the single biggest factor contributing to engagement, or more importantly the significant lack of it in the workplace. Both engagement and disengagement are choices - based on perceptions. Leaders have the ability to enhance perceptions, transforming disengaged employees into engaged team members.

According to many surveys, including Gallup's poll on engagement, we are facing an epidemic of disengaged people in the workplace. Some studies show that over 70% are not engaged; they are merely sleepwalking through work each day. Do you know people like this? Worse yet, 18% actively undermine their co-workers? Have you ever experienced this? Finally, close to half of the workforce are looking for new jobs.

The actual percentage of engaged workers, those who show up each day with positive attitudes and want to make strong contributions may be as low as 13%. If you have ever walked into a culture that lacks engagement, you may not be able to see it, but you can certainly feel it. How would you feel if the United States military, all 2 million men and women currently serving in the Army, Navy, Air Force, and Marines, only had 13% engagement in their troops?

When I ask this question, most people answer with "scared." But why are leaders not scared when it occurs in their workplace? We should be. The engagement levels in the military are the highest of any organization in the world. How do they do it? One thing that every branch of service has in common is this — they develop their people, at every level, as leaders. Even if no one is following them yet, they are developed to think and act as leaders.

Enhancing the perceptions of team members and other leaders is an all-the-time responsibility. But how do you influence people to look at things differently, and to perceive a win-win perspective? Developing your team and growing your organization is like building a great structure. You cannot expect it to remain standing when it has been built upon a weak foundation.

Unfortunately, many leaders attempt to do just that. They have visions of their "building" stretching into the skies and producing great results, but they spend very little time working on strengthening the foundation needed to support it all. If you were building a home, would it be worth your time to focus on building a strong foundation before you start putting up the walls? Absolutely!

Leadership Link Effectively leading your team will mean the difference between winning and losing.

BUILDING A STRONG FOUNDATION

Typically, you will not need to wear a hard hat while making *The LEADERSHIP Connection* at your organization. But understanding why building contractors start with a solid foundation for their buildings will provide great insight for leaders who strive to build and develop their organizations.

A solid foundation is designed to hold up and keep together the structure above it. A building built only on bare earth is more likely to become cracked and damaged over time. Furthermore, the ground is never quite still and, in many cases, not totally solid. A strong foundation increases the longevity of the building and ensures that it remains safer for the people inside of it.

The foundation of a building requires three critical elements to increase its strength: cement, sand, and water. The proper mixture of these elements creates concrete, which has been instrumental in creating structures such as the Hoover Dam and even the Coliseum of ancient Rome, which is still standing, nearly 2,000 years later. What makes up the foundation of your organization?

As a leader, the foundation, the enhanced perceptions – (Part I) you are establishing will help you to elevate priorities (Part II), empower people (Part III), and exceed possibilities (Part IV) in your organization. Like any given structure, each organization faces its own natural hazards, which can take a heavy toll on your "building" and your desired results.

The egos, attitudes, and varying personalities of your team can do significant damage, unless you create a strong foundation by enhancing their perceptions. To do this, you will need to combine three critical elements:

The Three Elements for a Strong Foundation:

1. Clearly Define Leadership

2. Develop a Unifying Culture

3. Identify Priority Goals

Most leaders struggle to understand why their team members are reluctant to help them build a better company. It is usually not that people have a lack of belief in the new direction, but rather a lack of faith in the current foundation. If you want the "buy-in" from your team, harness the power of creating a strong leadership foundation to help enhance their perceptions.

By paying particular attention to enhancing the perceptions of your team, you will establish a higher level of confidence, stability, and dedication. The toughest distance we travel, on our leadership expedition, is the six inches between our ears – how we perceive things. Consistently communicating the deeper meaning of leadership, culture, and goals will significantly enhance your ability to impact the way your team perceives things and their focus on achieving greater results.

IT ALL STARTS WITH THE LEADERS

People assigned to leadership positions typically possess a solid understanding of their industry and the products and services of their organizations. But to succeed as a leader, you will need much more than a knowledge of how the company functions. You must possess a deeper understanding of how to enhance the perceptions of your team – the six inches between their ears.

When I work with leaders on enhancing perceptions, I use a highly effective, state-of-the-art training tool – a 3x5 card. My sessions often begin by having the leaders in the room take a few minutes to clearly articulate three things for me. On the small blank card, they jot down their own definition of leadership, a brief description of the organization's culture, and the current goals of the company.

I give them only a minute to compile their thoughts, and as you might have already guessed, I receive a wide variety of answers. Many leaders struggle to articulate these three vital components. When a leader is unable to explain the foundation of their organization, why would anyone stand on it? Or stand for it?

If leaders cannot define "leadership," how can their team effectively follow them? They cannot! What happens if a leader struggles to describe the culture within the company, or worse yet, there is no discernible culture? Without a unifying culture, the team will experience a lack of identity, which often produces a lack of commitment and results.

Finally, I encounter leaders, who do not fully understand their organization's goals. Goals provide hope and give inspiration. They set a clear direction for the entire team. When a leader does not know the destination, how can anyone be expected to arrive there?

Imagine how much more confident you and your team will feel as leadership is defined, culture is unified, and goals are accomplished. Now, imagine how inspired your team will be to know that the foundation of your organization is strong, solid, and ready for growth.

As a leader, the meaning behind your message is paramount. "Why" you are doing something is usually far more important than "what" you are doing. But there is something far greater that your "Why?" – your Who! As we begin our expedition, we will focus on "Who" you are doing this for – the people on your team. By focusing on leadership, culture, and goals, your confidence and certainty will grow, and soon you will begin to enhance the perceptions of your team members and other leaders.

As you announce new plans and roll out new initiatives, silence will be replaced by the sound of a unified and excited team – a team ready to follow their leader. Always keep in mind that most people want to be a part of something great, something special, and something life-changing. Leaders ensure that their team members know the organization is moving in that direction and built on a solid foundation.

Only by enhancing the perceptions of the team will leaders create a shared language within their organization. Your success as a leader will ultimately rest on your ability to enhance the way your team views their circumstances, not just their environments. To start enhancing perceptions, let's take a closer look at defining leadership for your organization.

Chapter 1

Clearly Define Leadership

What Does it Mean to be a Leader?

What are some important elements to a successful marriage? Among many others, you would probably agree that love, trust, desire, respect, compassion, friendship, communication, and fidelity should be at the top of the list. What could happen if two people fell in love, married, but then discovered they had different definitions of what each of those words meant? What impact would it have on their relationship? Sadly, statistics show that over 50 percent of marriages will end in divorce.

While many factors could end a marriage, I believe most relationships begin to erode because the two people, who were once head-over-heels in love with each other, did not share the same definition of what it means to be married – they did not speak the same language. Most relationships begin with high levels of excitement and passion, but all of that can quickly fall apart if important aspects of their marriage are left open for interpretation.

When definitions are misunderstood, or worse yet, never established, the outcome is rarely positive. As a leader, the relationships you develop are paramount to your success. Inaccurate definitions can negatively affect your team, your peers, your leaders, your vendors, and your customers. You cannot afford to have important components of your business interpreted incorrectly. Yet many leaders only hope their team shares the same definitions. But *hope* is not a solid strategy for leaders.

THE IMPORTANCE OF LEADERSHIP

Regardless of what industry we work in, as leaders, we are all in the same *business* – the people business. While leaders speak fluently about their job duties, they tend to be at a loss for words when it comes to their leadership responsibilities. So, I have provided a quick *Latin Lesson* at the beginning of each chapter. Not only will you learn a new phrase or word, but I have found that it is easier to recall when it is in Latin. It also makes it sound more important!

LATIN LESSON

DUCTUS EXEMPLO

Lead by Example

As part of your new leadership language, we will continue to turn clichés into dynamic leadership statements. Ductus Exemplo (Lead by Example) is a common cliché that is mentioned because it sounds powerful. But rarely are there any actionable steps to do it. We have all heard this phrase and leaders are encouraged to do it daily, but most do not understand how to.

You will no longer have that problem because I have just activated a critical part of your brain – your reticular activating system (RAS). This is also known as your extrathalamic control modulatory system. The medical definition states that it is our set of connected nuclei, in our brains, that regulates wakefulness and sleep-wake transitions. In layman's terms, it helps us to notice certain things while we ignore other things.

Have you ever bought a new vehicle then immediately began seeing that same vehicle on the roads? Were people copying your sound buying techniques or were the vehicles always there? They were always there, but now that vehicle is important to you and your RAS allows the information into your brain.

Now, your RAS will allow in all of the leadership sights and sounds around you, that may have not been allowed in earlier. You have now become self-aware as a leader. Ductus Exemplo is the motto of the United States Marine Corps Office Candidate School, setting the bar high on all incoming Marine

Officers. Leading by example will cause us to be aware of every word, action, and gesture we make, allowing leadership to enter our minds.

Leadership Link When we lead by example, we help to align our perceptions with the perceptions of our team.

DEFINING LEADERSHIP FOR YOUR TEAM

The most important word you can define for your organization is "leadership." When I review the 3x5 cards from my sessions, I am amazed at the high level of variance in the definitions of this critical element. From junior leaders to senior executives, the meaning dramatically differs. No wonder individual members on the same leadership team often experience a wide-array of varying results. For a team to accomplish its objectives, the leaders must develop a shared meaning of leadership and what it means to be a leader in their organization.

But creating a definition can be a difficult task. Did you know that the Oxford English Dictionary currently contains 171,476 words? While we only use a small portion of these words daily, each one can have many different definitions. *Leadership* is no different. It has numerous meanings and perceptions. Depending on who you speak with, the word *leader* can have several different meanings.

- To a fisherman, a *leader* means: a short length of wire, or similar material by which a hook is attached to a fishing line.

- To a film editor, a *leader* means: a blank strip at the beginning or end of a film, used in threading or winding.

- To a plumber, a *leader* means: the section of a storm drain that guides water away from a roof.

All of these unique definitions are correct, especially if you fish, edit films, or install storm drains. But they will not help you to effectively lead your team and achieve the desired results you seek. To do so, you will need a meaningful, purpose-filled definition of what it means to be a leader in your organization.

It is imperative that leaders create their own unique interpretation of the word; one that will unify both the leaders and the team. Just as a marriage can begin to dissolve because of misunderstandings, many leaders experience a similar deterioration with their professional relationships by failing to establish a shared and consistent definition of leadership.

Leadership tends to have two distinct perspectives in most organizations. First is the perception of those doing the leading, and second, the perception of those being led. If you think the answers on the 3x5 cards, given by the leaders, have some head-scratching definitions, try asking employees to describe the level of leadership they are receiving. Make sure you give each of them more than one card because they usually have no shortage of constructive feedback about their leaders and their lack of leadership skills.

The importance of defining leadership in your company does not only help to support the current leaders, it benefits the entire team. Because the ability to accomplish your goals will be based on the combined efforts of the team members and the leaders, you must connect them all with a shared definition of leadership. When I look up the word *leadership*, which is in the top one percent of words searched in online dictionaries, the definition is a bit underwhelming: "holding the position or office of a leader."

Being said, we are all in a position of leadership. But that does not mean we all effectively lead our teams. This definition simply implies we have been appointed to a position requiring a leader. So, the big question becomes, "What is a leader?"

WHAT DOES IT MEAN TO BE A LEADER IN YOUR ORGANIZATION?

While many hold the title, most do not fully understand the importance of what it means to be a leader. Without a solid definition in place, you will fail to make the connection with your team, your leaders, and any other important relationships.

I have spent years developing my own personal definition of what I expect of myself as a leader. I keep it simple, direct, and free of misunderstandings. It is based on the concepts I learned in the Marine Corps, the skills I personally applied in the business sector, and the strategies I have successfully shared with thousands of leaders across the country. My definition constantly holds me to a higher standard. Your definition should, too.

To me, the word "lead" implies movement in a specified direction. So, you must have a clear vision of your desired destination. After all, as a leader you are going somewhere, right? The word "leader" suggests that people are following you, or at least they *should* be following you. So where are you leading them? In addition to articulating the destination, I clearly express what it will take for our team to arrive there. My definition of being a leader helps to energize and keep me focused.

It inspires me and my team to continually grow and become greater leaders. There are many traits, skills, theories, philosophies, techniques, and strategies about leading. But there is only one definition I use to distinguish myself as a leader.

THINK GREAT LEADER:

A person who clearly outlines a specified destination, and guides people there by course-correcting and adhering to the greater purpose behind the goals necessary for success.

Establishing what it means to be a leader is an exciting process. No longer are you looking to merely fill positions, you are seeking to fulfill expectations on a journey to greatness. You will be able to identify up-and-coming leaders on your team, and then create an environment of internal growth and personal development.

Leadership Link To be a successful leader, "Ego" must go.

THE TRAITS OF A GREAT LEADER

Although some people seem more natural at it, no one is born with leadership skills. Like everything else, leadership is a learned behavior. Many people are appointed to a leadership position, but do not possess the traits to lead.

When leadership is nothing more than a title, very little can be achieved. But important traits can be learned.

A good marriage might start by defining words such as love, respect, and fidelity. But a great marriage is experienced only when the qualities of both people meet their defined expectations. When someone fails to live up to these expectations, relationships dramatically suffer.

The qualities of a leader are always revealed through the traits they display. And their traits are quickly exhibited by what they say and what they do. Using the right leadership traits will help you to make a significant impact on the people you lead, ensuring you will achieve your desired results.

Your traits should embody your definition of leadership, allowing you to inspire, motivate, and move your team. But what is a trait? A trait is a distinguishing feature of a person's character. Through words and actions, traits reveal who a person truly is. Each time you communicate and every time you take an action, you display your traits, for all to experience.

Many organizations fail to identify the traits they expect of their leadership team, forcing some leaders to rely on their "good" intentions to navigate through challenging circumstances. The intentions of a leader last but a moment, but their words and actions will leave a permanent impression, positive or negative, on everyone they encounter.

How important are the words and actions of a leader? They are of great importance, so let's take a look at the traits that will help you to shine. To do that, we are going to examine the leadership traits of the U.S. Marine Corps.

14 LEADERSHIP TRAITS OF THE U.S. MARINE CORPS

Accepting a leadership position should be an exciting time. But it can also be a stressful experience. Most leaders are left to their own devices when it comes to establishing the "leadership" components of their position. New leaders might look to their job description to gain an understanding of what is expected, but these documents tend to outline their job duties, not their leadership expectations.

Since 1775, The Marine Corps has overcome insurmountable odds, endured great challenges, and survived life-threatening situations. They have done so in an ever-changing environment, and their leaders have successfully led their Marines through every conflict our country has faced; from the American Revolutionary War to the War on Terror.

The Marine Corps attributes their success to the leadership skills of their Marines, and they have dedicated their time and resources to help the men and women in their ranks to apply fourteen specific traits. I was introduced to these exact traits as a raw recruit in boot camp. Before my training was complete; before I learned how to fire my rifle; before I earned the title of U.S. Marine, these leadership seeds were planted in me.

I studied these concepts then, and still do today. In typical Marine Corps fashion, they use an acronym to help us identify, remember, and define these important traits: JJ DID TIE BUCKLE

JJ DID TIE BUCKLE

1.	Justice	Being fair and consistent.
2.	Judgment	Making the right decisions.
3.	Dependability	Your team should be able to rely on you.
4.	Initiative	Taking action, even without orders.
5.	Decisiveness	Make decisions without delay.
6.	Tact	How you treat people while delivering your message.
7.	Integrity	Be honest and truthful in what you say and do.
8.	Enthusiasm	Have a sincere interest in your duties.
9.	Bearing	The way you conduct and carry yourself.
10.	Unselfishness	Put the team above yourself. Give credit to others.
11.	Courage	Remaining calm while recognizing fear.
12.	Knowledge	Know your job, your team, and current events.
13.	Loyalty	Possess an unwavering devotion to your team.
14.	Endurance	The mental and physical stamina to stay on course.

Imagine what your leaders could accomplish as they adopt just a handful of these traits in your business. Imagine the impact on your entire team; your entire organization. Like me, you probably get a sense of excitement and newfound hope just by reading them. Wait until you apply them.

Keep in mind that no one is 100 percent perfect with each of these traits. Constantly strive to be better and continually encourage your team to embrace these qualities. You now have parameters to hold yourself and other leaders to a higher level.

By clearly defining what it means to be a leader in your organization, you will provide your leaders with a definitive understanding of their leadership role. Then, as you identify the traits expected of a leader, you will provide them with a substantial tool for setting and maintaining the highest levels of personal excellence within your organization.

LEADERS LEAVE A LASTING IMPRESSION

There is no such thing as a leader without challenges. But we are not defined by our difficult circumstances. We are however, defined by how we respond to those challenges. Great leaders always leave a lasting impression on the people they lead. In a leadership position, it is far easier to leave a negative impression than a positive one. As a leader, you are constantly under the microscope. Every action you take and every word you speak is closely scrutinized, analyzed, and interpreted.

Over thirty years later, I can still recall specific moments when my drill instructors enhanced my perception of "why" we were doing specific tasks and most importantly, "who" we were doing them for. The physical training in boot camp was very demanding, but our leaders consistently expressed the greater purpose behind our actions, and they exemplified the fourteen leadership traits. Before we began any physical activity, we were instructed to repeat, "The more we sweat in peace, the less we bleed in war."

A perception-changing statement indeed. No longer was I merely climbing over obstacles, running for miles, or performing endless calisthenics, I was working on improving my chances for survival in combat. My tasks took on a different meaning because my leaders pointed out the bigger picture involved – looking out for the Marine to my left and the Marine to my right. They left a lasting impression on every recruit in Platoon 1095.

Leadership Link The qualities of a leader must be in alignment with the traits expected of great leaders.

Defining what it means to be a leader in your organization is a powerful start. But to experience the benefits of this process, you and your leaders will need to understand and adopt the traits that make a leader great.

Clearly defining leadership is the first step to *Enhancing Perceptions.*

LEADERSHIP STEPS

CLEARLY DEFINE LEADERSHIP

Elite Leadership Step – Define "Leader"

- With your team, define what it means to be a leader in your organization. Start with "A leader is a person who..."

  Allow your key leaders to build a definition that represents what every leader in your organization should strive to exemplify.

Additional Steps

- **Off-Site:** Take a team member (on-one-one) for lunch or coffee. Get to know them on a deeper level than just work. Ask the tough question, "How can I be a better leader for you?"

- **Top Three Traits:** Have your leaders (yourself included) write down the top three traits they expect from a leader and rank yourselves on a scale of 1-10 (10 being best) of how well you exhibit these traits. Discuss ways to improve each ranking.

- **Challenges:** Identify your leadership challenges and discover the solutions so you and your leaders can experience the breakthroughs needed to lead your people to higher levels.

Chapter 2

Develop a Unifying Culture

Culture Follows the Leader.

Over the past twenty years, corporate *culture* has become an increasingly popular buzz phrase, with many leaders attributing their success to the benefits of creating and operating within a dynamic environment. The importance of culture cannot be understated, but it is often overlooked. Many leaders pay far too little attention to the impact their organization's culture has on their results.

Developing a unifying culture will help you to influence your leaders and your team members in many ways. But before you rush off to reap the benefits of a creating powerful environment, let's first understand what a culture is and what it will do for your organization.

As you already know, every word has many meanings. Culture is no different, and while most leaders fail to define it, others tend to accept the already-established environment within their organizations. Worse yet, some ignore it altogether. Like a block of clay, leaders must pay particular attention to their role in continually shaping, molding, and strengthening their culture.

Webster's dictionary defines culture as "a way of thinking, behaving, or working that exists in a place or organization." A company's culture is its model or style of operating, creating the mood of the company and determining how people interact with one another and work toward accomplishing goals together. Culture impacts every person who encounters it – your team, your vendors, and your customers.

Leadership Link Your culture is exactly at the level of your tolerance for poor performance.

THE IMPORTANCE OF CULTURE

When people travel abroad, it is not uncommon to hear their excitement in experiencing new "cultures." Since the beginning of human existence, our ancestors formed different societies – the essence of human civilization. They represent core beliefs, traditions, and have clearly defined rules and standards for behavior. But why? Like today, early human communities not only provided security, but they provided a sense of identity – people want to feel like they belong.

When surveyed, about 95% of people admit to wanting to be a part of something special and something great. Unfortunately, most workplace environments fail to deliver, and leaders are often left with a revolving door of people coming and going. Or, worse yet, people remain in a dismal culture and become highly disengaged. What represents your culture – your identity?

LATIN LESSON

Semper Fidelis

Always Faithful

Perhaps the first sign of culture I experienced in the Marine Corps was found in my recruiter's office. *Semper Fidelis* is the motto of the entire Marine Corps. Marines regularly greet each other with the shortened version: Semper Fi'. This phrase is an integral part of their identity and can be found everywhere: on their literature, posters, website, t-shirts, and on bumper stickers. I wanted to be a part of this.

The importance of culture in any company cannot be overlooked. It is the environment in which everything grows; good and bad – positive and negative. How important is culture to your team? How important is it to the Marines? It's so important that they gave theirs a name – a French name. So, you get an additional French lesson in this chapter.

FRENCH LESSON

Esprit de Corps

The Spirit of the Corps

Marines are constantly reminded of their heritage, their reputation, their identity – their culture. They are expected to conduct themselves with the Spirit of the Corps – the highest levels of excellence. They do not want to let down their fellow Marines. If you were to name your current culture, what would it be? If you were to name your desired culture, what would it be?

When I travel, I wear a Marine Corps pin as a calling card to other Marines. Whether I'm in an airport or a restaurant, I will often here a proud and hearty "Semper Fi'" or "Ooh Rah" from a fellow Marine who spots me. Although we have never met, we are never strangers because we share the same identity – we are a part of the same unifying culture.

CULTURE MATTERS

Why is culture so important to an organization? Because it has the ability to pull people together, to provide them with inner fortitude, and to build camaraderie. Most importantly, it has the power to enhance their perceptions. With an inspiring environment in place, team members will see the impossible as possible. They will develop a "can-do" attitude, and they will concentrate on the solutions for success, rather than dwell on the obstacles of failure.

When you set out to accomplish your organization's goals (Chapter 3), would you rather entrust them to a team operating in a strong environment or a weak one? Successful leaders accomplish goals, and surrounding every successful leader is a culture filled with energy, excitement, and enthusiasm.

Leadership Link The essence of culture is people, not profits. Invest more into your people and profits will follow.

Culture links people together on a much deeper level than a paycheck ever will. Too many business leaders attempt to capitalize on the benefits of incorporating culture into their organizations, but they rarely realize why culture truly matters. When you implement a culture only to increase your results, you will struggle. But when you develop a culture that unifies the members of your team, you will more easily achieve your desired results and open the door to new opportunities.

Developing a unifying culture is a formidable task, and there is no single formula for success. As a leader, one of the most important aspects of creating this type of environment is to encourage team members to embrace new ways of thinking; new ways of working together. Inevitably, an organization's goals will evolve from year to year, and leaders must ensure that their teams adapt and grow to meet the needs of those changes.

Regardless of what products and services your organization offers, remember you are in the people business, and culture is based on people. Corporate environments should not focus solely on policies, procedures, or even profits. It should emphasize values, principles, and character. This is what develops a unifying culture.

CULTURE SIGNS

Successful leaders keep their fingers on the pulse of their culture because a discouraging environment can do a significant amount of damage to an organization. Signs of a lackluster culture can include:

- No shared values
- Lack of trust
- A focus on the problems
- Failures are tolerated
- People are not enjoying their work

When a negative culture can take hold, people lose confidence in their team and in their leaders. This type of environment will make your job as a leader exponentially more challenging and will push you and your team further away from your goals. Consistently assessing your culture, and making the necessary course corrections, is critical to your success.

An organization's environment is comprised of many components; everything from dress code to room decor, and from paid vacations to performance reviews. When formulating their feelings about their environment, team members reflect on a wide array of elements.

What indicators should you monitor to gain a better understanding of your culture? While many methods are used to assess the status of an organization's environment, three main techniques are commonly used, but each has its limitations.

1. Historical data

2. Surveys

3. Observations

Historical data can be helpful in that it can show trends in employee absenteeism, performance, and turnover. It can also display customer relations, retention, and satisfaction. It could be fair to say an organization with high employee turnover does not have an inspiring culture. But that is not always the case. The Marine Corps has 64 percent turnover rate every four years, but their environment is so strong that Marines continue to uphold it even after their tour of duty is complete.

On the other hand, I have worked with many companies with long-term team members, but their culture is dismal. Some people stay on board for a paycheck – not for passion. While helpful, historical data may not accurately depict the complete story about your environment.

Surveys can also be beneficial, provided that the feedback you receive is truthful. Many team members do not express their real feelings, especially when they know their leaders will be privy to the information. In addition, most surveys tend to have set questions with set answers, not allowing the person taking the survey to pick a response that accurately represents how they truly feel about the question. While providing some insight, surveys can be perceived as impersonal and fail to describe the intricacies of your culture.

While observation is probably the most effective of the three, team members will more than likely behave at their best when they are being observed, especially by their leaders. Observation can provide you with valuable information about your culture, but it might not reflect the entire truth.

I have used all three techniques but found that one particular method provided me with the information I truly needed to assess the environment properly and make the necessary enhancements to develop a unifying culture: **personal interaction**.

Leadership Link Most people want to be part of something special and something great. Leaders give people that opportunity.

In Shakespeare's "Henry V," King Henry shed his royal attire and walked among his troops during the early morning. With the approaching battle of Agincourt just hours away, Henry goes in disguise and joins four ordinary soldiers as they sit around a fire. Facing near certain death, the men voice their concerns – not just about dying, but about King Henry's leadership.

It was here that Henry exhibited a powerful leadership skill in gathering valuable information about his culture. He listened. He went on to deliver one of the longest soliloquies that Shakespeare had ever written. Ultimately, Henry connects himself and his troops to his core values, and he enhanced their perception. He was victorious as a soldier and a leader.

While I do not recommend you go in disguise to discover the truth from your team members, I do emphasize that leadership is a people business and leaders need to spend more time interacting with their people. Too many leaders talk to their team members only when something goes wrong. Look for opportunities to speak with them about what they are doing right and invest the time necessary to build their trust and improve your culture.

As you open lines of communication, your team will share the important information you need to know about your environment, from a point of view you might not often see. I attained my most valuable information over lunches and coffees, typically out of the office. Investing the necessary one-on-one time with your team will provide a huge return.

CULTURE ASSESSMENT

As leaders, we must pay close attention to our culture, especially if we intend on accomplishing things through the efforts of others. I have discovered that leadership will flourish, and people will grow beyond the limitations of an organization if the culture is unifying. An environment that supports great growth occurs when you and your team maintain high levels of five specific elements - The Leadership Vowels.

The Leadership Vowels:

A	Attitude
E	Excellence
I	Initiative
O	Outcome
U	Unwavering

When these five conditions are present and at the right levels, high performance will flourish. Let's take a closer look at each category so we can use these five characteristics to quickly assess the culture within your organization. The following descriptions, listed for each Leadership Vowel, represent a 10 out of 10, on a scale of 1 to 10.

Attitude

Both positive and negative attitudes are highly contagious. Does everyone bring their A-game – everyday? Do they conduct themselves with the highest levels of enthusiasm, being a beacon of positivity for other team members, regardless of their circumstances? That is a 10.

Excellence

Is your team dedicated to delivering the highest levels of customer and team satisfaction? Do they actually deliver? Good is not good enough, when great is attainable. Do they get the job done right the first time every time? That is a 10.

Initiative

Does everyone do what needs to be done without being told over and over? When no one is looking, does your team take care of their duties and responsibilities? Do they consistently ask their leaders and fellow team members, "What can I do for you?" That is a 10.

Outcome

Does everything serve a purpose? Is there an outcome for every meeting, all forms of communication, steps in the workflow, and team member reviews? Most importantly, does everyone on your team understand the outcome for the actions they take each day? That is a 10.

Unwavering

Does your team display the highest levels of commitment regardless of the challenges they face? Do they represent your organization by knowing and fulfilling the mission statement, vision statement, and core values? Do they fully embrace your identity? That is a 10.

Now that you understand my criteria for a 10, you can honestly assess your leadership team, individual departments, or the organization as a whole by ranking each vowel on a scale of 1 to 10 (10 being highest).

Culture Assessment:

A	Attitude	_____
E	Excellence	_____
I	Initiative	_____
O	Outcome	_____
U	Unwavering	_____

Add up your total score. Where did your culture rank with a possible score of 50? How does your culture impact the performance of your people?

0-25	Culture is Withering	- hindering performance
26-40	Culture is Supporting	- sustaining performance
41-50	Culture is UNIFYING	- magnifying performance

To put your mind at ease, know that most leaders rank their cultures between 25 and 30 for the first assessment.

ENHANCING YOUR CULTURE

Assessing culture is one thing; enhancing it is another. It takes time, patience, and persistency for a leader to shape an organization's environment. While the multiple elements that identify a culture are unique among each organization, some common denominators help to support unifying cultures.

Dress code, room colors, and the lounge amenities might shape people's perceptions, but I have found three distinct components that resonate deeper with every team member and every leader. These elements will help to develop the unifying culture your team needs to succeed. They also help to answer three important questions: Who? How? What?

The Three Elements of a Unifying Culture:

1. The Big Picture   – Who?

2. The Style   – How?

3. The Opportunity   – What?

THE BIG PICTURE – WHO?

Identifying why your organization exists is important. Is your organization bigger than its products and services? Leaders help to develop and continually share their organization's Big Picture – everything that represents your company, inside and outside.

Inside: includes mission and vision statements, core values, and brand statements to help create a unique identity for the team. Successful leaders harness the power of this identity to move the team forward.

- *Mission*: your organization's current purpose – what needs to be accomplished each day.

- *Vision*: your organization's future objectives – what your organization will be in the next five years.

- *Core Values*: your main principles that support your mission and vision.

- *Brand Statement*: A marketing tool that encompasses your organization's essence and reputation.

Most organizations identify themselves to their team members and customers by using one or more, or a combination, of the above definitions. Ultimately, what you are striving for is to create a "Who" statement. Let people know more of "who" your organization is; who the people are. A leader ensures that the organization's identity is brought to life and does not end up as mere words on a sheet of paper.

Leadership Link Create a culture that is all about the people – the Who!

Outside: great organizations do great things beyond their office walls. They give back to their communities and to the greater good. Serving in the Marine Corps gave me a tremendous sense of pride and self-worth, but not just because of our accomplishment on the battlefields. Marines also help children in their communities – their little Who's.

The Marine Corps launched their famous Toys for Tots program in 1947, and they have collected and delivered over 500,000,000 toys to children since then. This program gives each Marine, and their families, something to take part in for the greater good of their communities. It also develops a deeper sense of pride and satisfaction.

As a leader, provide your team with the opportunity to do something greater than fulfill their job descriptions. Provide them with an opportunity to grow outside of your organization as well as inside.

THE STYLE – HOW?

What your company does is important and *who* it does it for is even more important. But *how* it does it speaks volumes about the culture of your organization. The style in which your organization processes business, makes its products, and delivers its services can be summed up as *how* it delivers. All of the branches of the armed services defend our nation, but *how* they do it is different. Their *how* is a defining part of their culture.

I can say from experience that most organizations do not lack the ability to design a proper workflow or process. They understand what needs to happen at Point A, and what needs to happen at Point B. However, most leaders fall short when it comes to implementing the uniqueness that defines their organization – their systems.

Systems can unify departments or build walls between them. It can improve communication among team members or completely silence them. The right systems can improve cooperation or increase resentment. Most people do not leave an organization because they dislike what the company does, they leave because they do not like the way things are done.

Does this sound familiar? "It was operations fault," said the sales team. "It was the sales department's responsibility," cried the operations team. When you have contention between departments, look closely at your systems, and ensure that they unify your team and promote exceptional communication.

Ultimately, your *how* helps to make your company memorable; to your team and to your customers. Every step in a defined system needs an individual or department to be held accountable (Chapter 6). It requires team members to communicate (Chapter 7), and positions leaders to pay greater attention to making sure that all the gears are turning properly.

THE OPPORTUNITY – WHAT?

Growth is a crucial component of every organization. Sales growth, customer satisfaction growth, and team growth are all paramount. If a company is not growing, it is dying. Leaders are appointed to help facilitate all areas of growth within their organizations. But the problem is that too many leaders only focus on growth. I know, focusing on growth sounds like a good thing. But there is much more...

While team members might listen to you speak about growth, they are ultimately waiting to hear about the opportunity. Here's an important acronym I learned in the Marine Corps: WIIFM – What's In It For Me? Even in an organization with the highest levels of teamwork and unselfishness, Marine Corps leaders do not overlook the importance of ensuring that their team members benefit.

What is in it for your people? Do they know? People often leave growing organizations because they feel left out; perceiving that the company benefitted from their efforts, but they did not. Never make the mistake that people should just be happy to have a job. Great leaders constantly find ways to provide incentives, promotions, and enhancements as the organization grows.

Leadership Link Successful leaders achieve growth for the company while providing opportunities for their people!

YOUR CULTURE - UNIFIED

Without a defined culture, leaders struggle to maximize their potential as well as the potential of their team members. Simultaneously, they minimize opportunities for the growth of their organization. By focusing on and sharing the big picture, the style, and the opportunities available, you will develop a unifying culture that will dramatically increase your results.

Leadership Link Unifying your culture is a critical step for enhancing perceptions.

As your company grows, a positive, supportive environment will help to keep it flourishing. It will enable you to retain strong team members, weed out weak ones, and attract new energetic people for future growth. When a culture is positive and inspiring, each team member will share a common purpose with the activities required to help promote sustainable growth.

Most importantly, a unifying culture will allow the team to experience a sense of dedication and excitement toward accomplishing the goals necessary for success.

LEADERSHIP STEPS

DEVELOP A UNIFYING CULTURE

Elite Leadership Step – Enhance your Culture

- Rank each Leadership Vowel on a scale of 1-10 (10 being best) to assess your current culture. Next, identify ways to enhance each vowel.

			Rank	How to ENHANCE
•	**A**	Attitude	_____	_____
•	**E**	Excellence	_____	_____
•	**I**	Initiative	_____	_____
•	**O**	Outcome	_____	_____
•	**U**	Unwavering	_____	_____

Additional Steps

- **Describe Desired Culture:** Identify the words that represent your ideal environment, like engaging, supportive, exciting, productive, and fun.

- **Identity:** Call a Leadership Meeting to discuss your current forms of identity: Mission Statement, Vision Statement, Core Values, and any other components. Can they be enhanced or used more often?

- **Community:** Share the ways your organization makes a difference in the community. This lets the team know that you are bigger than your company. Perhaps you support specific charity organizations. Perhaps you need to.

Chapter 3

Identify Priority Goals

A Leader Without Goals is like a Ship Without a Rudder.

The way your team perceives your organization is the way they present your organization; to each other and to your customers. By clearly defining what it means to be a leader (Chapter 1) and developing a unifying culture for your team (Chapter 2), you have already started to enhance their perceptions. One additional component will help you to dramatically enhance the way people view your company and their role in it.

Many leaders fail to see the value of investing the time necessary to identify goals for their business. Whether it is the department manager who has too much on his or her plate, the high-level executive with years of experience, or the business owner who believes he or she already has all the answers, most miss the opportunity of incorporating game-changing goals into their workplace.

Priority goals are necessary for a business to grow. They are the most effective way to decide how to move forward, and how to stay on the right path to achieve greater results. The accomplishment of those goals will help to increase trust, belief levels, and motivation throughout the entire organization. Goals are much more critical than most leaders realize.

THE IMPORTANCE OF GOALS

Preparing their service members for long deployments, I have shared my goal-setting strategies for many commands in the Armed Services. Understanding the positive impact of setting and accomplishing goals, military leaders emphasize that their troops and their families set meaningful goals together.

With divorce rates, depression, and suicide rates at critically high levels, I did not take lightly my opportunity to share the strategies and techniques, from my book, *The GOAL Formula*, with service members and their families. I gave a goal-setting presentation in Northern California to the Yellow Ribbon Reintegration Program (YRRP). The YRRP is part of the Air National Guard and they hold events for service members and their spouses, before and after deployments.

In their literature, the YRRP encourages goal-setting, especially during stressful times. In the Family Deployment Information Guide, for the US Navy, it encourages couples to engage in goal-setting by stating, "Both of you may want to consider setting some personal goals to accomplish during the deployment. Examples include: quit smoking, start a hobby, learn a new skill, or continue education."

There is even an article on Military.com that says to, "Set some personal goals to work toward during the deployment. You'll find you are better prepared to handle the stress of separation and take care of yourself and your family." With critical missions at hand, military leaders understand the deeper power of setting and accomplishing goals – it enhances perceptions.

In the business world, there are very few things that could be considered as stressful as deploying for combat. Yet, most leaders fail to implement goal-setting as a strategy to support their people through the challenges they face each day. This is a critical mistake. Imagine what it would be like to work in an environment where everyone is focused on accomplishing priority goals. Imagine if everyone maximized each day to do so.

LATIN LESSON

CARPE DIEM

Seize the Day

Easily the most popular Latin phrase, *Carpe diem* dates back to the Roman poet Horace (23 BC). The literal translation suggests that he was encouraging people to "pluck the day" – looking at each day as a ripe piece of fruit. I believe that Horace was encouraging us to take hold of what each day presents to better prepare for the future. When leaders fail to use goals with their team members, it is like letting ripe fruit fall to the ground and rot.

Setting and accomplishing goals is easier than most think. But without a *GOAL Formula*, we miss the ripe fruit within our grasp. According to a study by the University of Scranton, shared by Inc.com, about 92% of people fail at their goals. When you consider all the life-changing goals set each year, that is a staggering number to comprehend. When you consider all the people who could have been positively impacted by the accomplishment of these goals, it feels even worse.

If that number holds true, then that leaves only 8% who consistently accomplish their goals. As leaders we need to transform our teams into the 8 Percenters! Understanding how to set, accomplish, and exceed goals is paramount for any leader who wants to achieve greater results. To succeed, we must take control of each day... for it is ripe!

UNDERSTANDING GOALS

Leaders have countless excuses why they fail to set goals. But there is one, rock-solid reason to firmly establish them: they significantly enhance perceptions. How do goals help to enhance perceptions? Priority goals give hope and inspire. They promote forward-thinking, creating high-levels of camaraderie, loyalty, and teamwork. As you share the Big Picture of your organization with your team, goals will give them purpose, far beyond their job descriptions.

Every accomplished goal moves you and your team one step closer to the grand vision of your company. Leaders must pay close attention to developing a culture that will support the accomplishment of the goals necessary for growth. Remember, leaders guide their teams in a "specified direction." The goals you set and accomplish are milestones on the path to the destination. Identify priority goals, and then pour resources into the achievement of these vital objectives.

Setting and accomplishing goals are two completely different things. Most organizations fall short in their efforts because they lack a detailed understanding of how and why they need to accomplish goals in their environment. Understanding three essential elements will dramatically increase your ability to set and accomplish priority goals, while simultaneously enhancing the perceptions of your entire team.

Three Essential Elements of Priority Goals:

1. The Types

2. The Effect

3. The Formula

GOALS ARE NOT TASKS

I often meet leaders who confuse goals with tasks. In order to accomplish priority goals in your organization, many important tasks will be associated with them. Tasks make up the individual duties required for accomplishing each of your goals. But there is a significant difference between goals and tasks.

While most people find a sense of satisfaction after a task has been completed, that feeling is usually temporary and quickly fades away. Goals are different. The satisfaction gained from accomplishing a goal is long-lasting, providing inspiration and positive energy. Another significant difference is that you do not have to wait until a goal is accomplished to receive the full benefit. Tasks are important. Goals are a priority.

Moving forward with your goals increases the performance and enhances the perceptions of everyone involved. Leaders are often a bit hesitant about setting goals for their teams, departments, and organizations, which makes sense when 92% of people fail at their goals. In addition, the idea of setting goals seems daunting, especially when thousands of possible goals could qualify as a "priority" to an organization's growth. So where do you start?

Leadership Link Set goals to establish a clear understanding of where you are going, so people want to follow you.

TYPES OF GOALS

Your perception of goals is the best place to begin. Most leaders use goals as a way to keep their organization alive. But being alive and growing are far different. If your organization needs a monthly revenue of $500,000 to "keep the lights on," then $500,000 might seem like a good goal to hit each month. But most team members look at these types of goals as unfulfilling quotas.

Priority goals, however, help an organization to break beyond the status quo and enable it to move upward, toward greater results. They inspire team members and encourage them to unleash their true potential. They allow people to see themselves differently.

Goals give power. They are like the engine of a vehicle, more specifically, a six-piston engine. Why an engine? Because your organization is a vehicle. And that vehicle has been built to move forward, heading in a direction that will arrive at a GREAT destination. Priority goals are the pistons of that engine. They provide unlimited sources of power and energy to your team. But to achieve maximum performance, it is crucial that all pistons operate and fire in unison.

I have had the privilege of collaborating directly with leaders from hundreds of different organizations and industries. Working with each of them has provided me the opportunity to be involved with thousands of unique goals that move their organizations upward.

While the goals themselves might have been slightly different in scope and size, I discovered that virtually every goal fell into six categories. To successfully accomplish a goal in one category, make the link between the other five.

Types of Goals:

1. Financial

2. Customer

3. Team

4. Operational

5. Marketing

6. Community

FINANCIAL GOALS

• These goals help to assess an organization's performance. Establishing and monitoring measurable financial goals, like sales goals, will help to increase earnings and profit margins, while also allowing for more effective budgeting.

• Financial goals can be established based on benchmarking the "best-in-industry" as well as your own organization's historical performance.

• Examples of common financial goals are: increase revenue by 25 percent, improve profit margins by 10 percent, and reduce unnecessary expenses by 5 percent.

• Most organizations tend to focus only on financial goals, feeling that accomplishing these goals will solve all of their problems. Financial goals are only one piston in your engine.

CUSTOMER GOALS

• These goals help to increase customer retention, expand your customer base through referrals, and improve relationships between team members and customers.

• Customer goals help your organization to measure its progress toward achieving the highest levels of customer satisfaction, which will have a direct impact on the success of your financial goals. Customer goals establish performance standards and help to develop improvement programs for team members and leaders.

• Examples of common customer goals are: reducing order errors by 50 percent, developing loyalty programs, and establishing consistent communication with the current customer base.

- Accomplishing customer goals will help to influence the customer's perception of your team and your organization.

- Most organizations can immediately identify the customer goals needed to improve their results, but they often fail to implement the company-wide steps necessary to guarantee long-term success.

TEAM GOALS

- These goals build loyalty, inspire creativity, increase morale, and decrease complaining. Team goals emphasize the "opportunity" that develops from the "growth" of your organization.

- Team goals announce to your staff that they are a priority, not just another cog in the wheel. They also promote high levels of personal and professional development within your organization.

- Examples of important team goals are: setting up financial rewards, establishing educational programs, and opening more opportunities for promotion.

- Most leaders only consider team goals as a way to raise morale, so their team members perform better. Effective team goals place an emphasis on the personal and professional development of the team.

OPERATIONAL GOALS

- These goals increase effectiveness and efficiency, by focusing on the improvement of the workflow and communication within your organization. These goals will increase productivity while decreasing mistakes.

- Operational goals are best accomplished by having team members involved in the development, implementation, and maintenance of these necessary priorities.

- Examples of key operational goals are: revising the procedures within your workflow system (checkpoints, order forms, reports), streamlining internal communication, and setting up consistent benchmarks to track the results of your goals. Benchmarks allow you to follow the timeframes needed to complete a transaction, as well as analyzing the type/frequency of errors.

- Most leaders make a significant mistake by failing to set operational goals, robbing themselves of the valuable information needed to make urgent course-corrections. They attempt to navigate through the sub-par systems already in place, instead of investing the time necessary for accomplishing their operational goals.

- Accomplishing these goals will allow you to improve your chances for hitting your customer goals. Making consistent improvements to the way you do business, will open the door to doing more business.

MARKETING GOALS

- These goals will increase your social media reach, elevate web traffic, and improve results from advertising campaigns. They create excitement and influence existing customers, as well as potential new customers, to take a closer look at everything your organization has to offer.

- Marketing goals should include the input from your entire team. Their involvement will increase their buy-in and make them feel like an integral part of the organization as it grows and reaches new heights.

- Examples of important marketing goals are: developing or enhancing your mission and vision statements, creating a brand statement, launching a new version of the website, and starting a "contacting campaign" to deliver a new message to customers.

- Most organizations understand the value of important marketing goals but fail to ever experience their benefits. I believe this is due in part to the perceived expense associated with marketing initiatives. The above-mentioned marketing goals provide a way to enhance your marketing, while supporting your financial goals, without investing significant amounts of money.

COMMUNITY GOALS

- These goals help to leave a lasting impact in the lives of everyone your organization touches – far more than any product or service ever will.

- Community goals provide your team with a greater sense of purpose, achievement, and fulfillment. Community goals bond team members, leaders, customers, and vendors. They also have the power of introducing to your organization, people who might have never had the opportunity of connecting before.

- Examples of community goals are: raising money for specific charities, creating volunteer teams to participate in community events, and establishing "green" objectives that will have a positive impact on our global environment, such as minimizing the use of paper, within your organization.

- Most organizations do not invest the time necessary to identify relevant community goals. But the results of these goals might create the deepest sense of commitment and loyalty from your team, increasing their desire to help accomplish all of your other goals.

Leadership Link Challenge yourself to identify at least one goal in each category that would be a priority to your organization.

THE IMPACT OF GOALS

Setting and accomplishing priority goals will have a significant impact on the perceptions of your team. Whether that outlook is positive or negative is up to you. Leaders are often dismayed when their staff fails to embrace the goals that have been set, even when the accomplishment of those goals will provide high levels of corporate growth.

How can the goals of your organization create a positive impact for your team? I have discovered three ways to ensure that the right impact occurs with each priority goal.

Three ways to Increase the Impact of Goals:

1. Enlist the help of your team

2. Show your team the benefits

3. Harness the power of teamwork

Enlist the Help of Your Team

I find it ironic that goal-setting typically involves only the senior leadership team. But the accomplishment of the goals, that will significantly enhance the results of the organization, fall onto the entire team. I cannot overstate the importance of their involvement in the goal-setting process.

Team members who actively participate in this process are more likely to enthusiastically participate in the goal-accomplishing process. Enlisting their help not only increases their buy-in, but team members often provide an insight that can be helpful in the development of additional goals.

Show Your Team the Benefits

Your team members have likely joined your company for a variety of reasons. But their decision to stay, and more importantly, to become a powerful contributor, will be based on the opportunities available to them through the accomplishment of goals. Successful leaders make the link between the growth of their organization and the benefits for their team.

When someone benefits from a goal, he or she takes ownership of that goal. Ultimately, people are motivated by factors that directly and positively impact their careers and personal lives. But what goals do people care most about? No, they are not listed in six types of goals for your business. They care most about their own personal goals. Great leaders never forget about their *Who*. They earn the right to learn the personal goals of their team members, and support them, as the organization accomplishes its priority goals.

Harness the Power of Teamwork

Priority goals unify a team. Team members who work together to accomplish the goals that will benefit their organization and their personal lives will develop a kindred spirit. Shared goals bring people together, and help to build the camaraderie needed, to not only accomplish each goal but to exceed them, even when facing challenges.

Co-created goals increase the level of buy-in you receive from your team. By increasing the number of people who will benefit from accomplishing these goals, you will increase the level of teamwork. Highly-motivated team members have a willingness to get the job done efficiently and effectively, creating greater results and higher levels of success.

Leadership Discover the deeper, meaningful personal goals that your team
Link members have for their lives.

THE FORMULA FOR ACCOMPLISHING GOALS

Taking on new goals might seem like a daunting task. People often feel overwhelmed at the thought of the required tasks, as well as the additional efforts necessary to ensure each goal is realized. Understanding the formula needed to accomplish each goal is critical. In addition to providing structure and accountability, it will help to balance the energy required for success.

When it comes to accomplishing goals, I could write an entire book on this subject. Wait a minute – I have. As the author of *The GOAL Formula*, I regularly share the strategies and techniques from my book to help individuals and organizations accomplish priority goals. The formula is simple – there are just three elements to accomplishing your goals.

The GOAL Formula

STEPS + TIME + PEOPLE
=
ACCOMPLISHED GOALS

It's all about the *steps* you take (five), the *time* you allocate (90 days), and the *people* you enlist to support you. While I am not delving into each element of the formula, I am going to provide an explanation of the steps I use to accomplish all of my personal and professional goals.

As you might have noticed, I have a passion for the word *GREAT*. With my military background, I also have a fondness for acronyms. Let's take a closer look at the acronym G.R.E.A.T. to illustrate the five steps required.

The 5 GREAT Steps to Accomplishing Goals:

Goals   — Identify priority **G**oals

Reasons   — Establish powerful **R**easons

Expectations — Set high **E**xpectations

Actions   — Take all of the **A**ctions necessary

Tracking   — Intensely **T**rack your results

When you concentrate your efforts (the five steps) in a well–defined block of time, and also enlist the support of others, you will set and accomplish priority short–term and long–term goals, increase your results, and experience new levels of success.

For more information on *The GOAL Formula*, visit my website: www.thinkgreat90.com

Identifying and accomplishing goals is an educational process for leaders, helping them to realize what is necessary for the growth of their organization. Most businesses only need small adjustments to their engines, not a major overhaul. Leaders who make minor modifications will make major impacts with their goals.

By linking together, the six types of goals, ensuring that these goals have a positive impact, and by taking the necessary steps to accomplishing goals, you will not only realize your potential, but you will experience a dramatic enhancement in your perception and the perceptions of your team. You will also increase your ability to elevate priorities.

LEADERSHIP STEPS

Identify Priority Goals

Elite Leadership Step – *Who* Statement

- Identify what is most important to you, your team, and your company. What is your *Big Picture*, from which you will identify all your goals? Why are you doing what you do? Most importantly, *Who* do you want to impact and what is that impact?

Additional Steps

- **Personal Goals:** Get off-site with team members to better understand their personal goals – the goals that inspire them at the highest levels.

- **Priority Goals:** Identify the short-term goals that need to be accomplished in the next year and what quarter each should be reached.

- **90-Days:** Create a sense of urgency by placing each short-term goal into *The GOAL Formula*. Steps = GREAT. Then schedule the objectives that need to be accomplished in the next 90 days. Finally, enlist the support of key team members to support the accomplishment of each goal.

  - **G**   Goals   _____
  - **R**   Reasons   _____
  - **E**   Expectations   _____
  - **A**   Actions   _____
  - **T**   Tracking   _____

Part II

Elevate Priorities

Part II

Elevate Priorities

Focus "ON" Your Growth and Success.

The first three chapters of this book allowed us to step into the shallow end of the leadership pool as we concentrated on the six inches between people's ears, their perceptions. Part II, and the three subsequent chapters, will take us into the deep end of the leadership pool. This is where some of the more challenging work will begin, but the greatest rewards will occur. You will no longer be treading water as a leader, you will effectively swim.

Is it possible for an object to move up and down at the same time? If you are a leader who has not learned how to effectively elevate priorities within your organization, you might often experience this phenomenon, which defies all laws of physics as well as the essence of leadership. Perhaps you have enjoyed the overwhelmingly positive feelings of rising up as a leader, while simultaneously experiencing that downward, sinking feeling of having too much on your plate.

As a coach, my primary audience members are leaders with full plates and unforgiving time constraints. Whether I train them one-on-one, as part of a team, or in front of hundreds at a workshop, they have all experienced the feeling of rising and falling at the same time.

When a leader fails to prioritize their leadership responsibilities, the key elements to growing their organization, they will experience high levels of frustration, stress, and disappointment. One of the greatest hazards faced by leaders is being pulled in too many directions. Your leadership position should not be a dumping ground of unaccomplished projects, but rather a fine-tuned factory of growth-oriented priorities.

From the moment you accept the position of leadership, every task, big and small, seems to become a hot rush, with the lion's share of the work resting on your shoulders. Projects that had been put on the back burner, miraculously find their way onto your desk as urgent, "Stop everything you're doing" emergencies.

Within three months of working at the post-production company in the entertainment industry, I earned my first leadership position. No sooner, I had heaped on my desk, schedules, supplies, new hires, expenses, marketing, sales, etc. The list could go on and on, and it often does for most leaders. But I quickly learned that if everything is perceived as a "priority," then nothing is a true priority, and very little will be achieved.

THE IMPORTANCE OF PRIORITIES

Because we all wear many hats as leaders, we need to focus on our priorities. There are many activities on our plate, many of which may not be in our job descriptions. Below is a short list of some key elements that consume the time of many leaders.

• Meetings	• Reviews
• Interviewing	• Marketing
• Hiring	• Planning
• Write-Ups	• Training
• Firing	• Problems
• Shift Schedules	• Budgets
• Reports	• Workflow

We know this list could go on and on. Therefore, we need to consistently *Elevate Priorities*. To do that, we need to acknowledge that there is a significant difference between a calendar and a schedule. A calendar lets you know what day is coming. A schedule allows you to control what you do with each day. There is also a huge difference between priority and important.

Leadership Link Harness the power of your day by scheduling your priorities first.

BUSY VS. PRODUCTIVE

Based on the high levels of disengagement in the workplace, it is not a surprise that the impact can be felt in the performance of our people. When I meet with leaders, I often ask a simple question, "Could your people be more productive?" The answer is undeniably always, "Yes." I have never had a leader say, "No, my team is already performing at the highest levels of productivity all day."

By working with my clients, in their workplaces, I have discovered that most people are "busy" 100% of the day but are only productive about 20%. I am going to say something controversial, but here it goes. "Busy" is code for "I'm not engaged." After all, what is busy-work? Most people describe it as meaningless, non-important work. As leaders, we need to speak like leaders. I am never *busy*. When my plate is full, I either have a productive schedule or action-packed day.

Many people say they cannot help out or take on another task because they are "too busy." No one ever says, "I can't help because I'm too productive." Busy sends a powerfully negative message. We need our people to be productive. With 80% of each team member's day that could be more productive, that is a tremendous amount of time we have to work with. I'm not saying that you will transform every second of the day into critically productive time, but what would the impact be if you could get them to be productive 40% of their day, not just 20%?

Leadership Link Leaders strive to transform "busy" employees into "productive" leaders.

CREATE A SENSE OF URGENCY

Every organization is unique, consisting of vastly different goals for their overall strategic plan. Leaders must create a sense of urgency in order to elevate the priorities necessary for successful growth. While every action, task, and function performed within your organization should be important, and serve a specific purpose, not everything is a priority.

So how do you identify what is a priority and what is not? Fortunately, it is quite simple. Each day there are thousands upon thousands of actions that occur in any business. Orders are placed, negativity is spread, calls are made, forms are completed, meetings are conducted, team members are trained, new sales are made, and shift schedules are filled. Regardless of what action takes place, they all fall into one of three buckets.

I use three simple words to help make the distinction between the three buckets: OUT, IN, and ON. These hold the negative, important, and priority elements within an organization. What's in your buckets?

OUT   – Negative actions that weaken your organization

IN   – Important tasks that support your organization

ON   – Priority objectives that grow your organization

Successful leaders must be able to identify each of these elements, and also have a plan to remove, improve, or elevate each. While it might seem like common sense, far too many leaders fail to remove the elements that have no place in their businesses – the OUT's. These will do significant damage to their organization, and also to their reputation as a leader.

- "OUT" actions can range from derogatory discussions among your staff about other team members, leaders, and departments to unnecessary, time-consuming steps in your workflow.

- "OUT" actions are a result of weak leadership and a lackluster culture, resulting in a tremendous amount of wasted time, and a deep-seated resentment throughout the entire organization. These actions make it difficult to effectively lead your people and virtually impossible to grow your organization. Like a virus, negative actions will continue to grow unless they are properly treated.

I find it interesting that people who routinely say they are "Too busy," somehow find the time to participate in OUT actions. So, one of the first priorities of a leader is to identify and remove any "OUT" actions from your organization. As you enhance perceptions by clearly defining leadership, developing a unifying culture, and identifying priority goals, you will find that many, who have mastered the "OUT" actions, may start to leave your team.

As you elevate priorities, you will encourage and influence others to turn their attention to the "IN" and "ON" elements necessary for stability and growth. While most leaders would quickly agree that their efforts should focus "ON" the business, rather than "IN" the business, they struggle to clearly articulate the difference between the two concepts.

- "IN" activities are vitally important, helping to support your organization's mission.

- "ON" activities move you closer to the priority goals; those that help to develop the enhanced perceptions to achieve your vision.

Everything you do as a leader makes powerful connections, if you continue to link up the "ON" objectives necessary for success. Leaders must strive to transfer their efforts from "IN" the business to "ON" the business.

For most of the leaders I have surveyed, the unfortunate ratio of "IN" vs. "ON" typically starts at about 90 percent "IN" vs. 10 percent "ON." When a leader can only allocate 10 percent of his or her time to the priorities necessary for growth, what results can be expected?

Leadership Link Enhance your language as a leader and move from busy to productive.

HITTING THE TARGET

To elevate your priorities, which will help to stop the sinking feeling most leaders experience, let's take a closer look at "IN" vs. "ON." It is critical to make the distinction between these two elements, and to do so, let's go back to 1987, when I was a raw recruit in Marine Corps boot camp. Sporting freshly shaved heads and wearing brand new camouflage uniforms, Platoon 1095 marched to the armory in our all-leather combat boots, which were still not broken in.

The excitement of being issued our M-16A2 Assault Rifles was more than enough to help block out the pain from the fresh blisters on our feet. Being handed our weapons was one thing but mastering them would bring each recruit one step closer to our life-changing goal: earning the title of U.S. Marine. Because every Marine is a rifleman, regardless of what our job specialty is, this day had a high level of intensity. We were enthusiastic and nervous at the same time. Have you ever felt like that?

From the moment my hands grasped my rifle, I began to understand the difference between important tasks and priority objectives. Having a much deeper understanding of both, our drill instructors created a sense of urgency for each. After hours of classroom training, endlessly practicing our breathing and aiming techniques, and repetitively firing hundreds of live rounds on the rifle range, we mastered every aspect about "how" our rifles worked.

We possessed an extensive knowledge about the important tasks (IN) that we needed to operate our weapon. In less than a minute, we could disassemble and reassemble it, clean it to the point of looking like it had just come off the assembly line, and we could march in perfect unison with it as if it were an extension of our own bodies. For a Marine, these are certainly important tasks.

But our priority objective (ON) with this weapon was to fire it accurately in combat. To elevate this priority, our drill instructors used three distinct techniques.

- They set high *expectations* for our performance.
- They would *delegate* specific portions of our rifle training to our Primary Marksmanship Instructors (PMIs).
- They held us *accountable*, tracking every shot we fired.

Our drill instructors taught us more than just "how" to accurately hit a target from 500 yards away. They taught us "why" we needed to become proficient with our weapons. In a combat situation, our rifles could mean the difference between making it home from deployment, or having a flag sent home to be presented to our family. It could mean the difference between saving the Marines to your left and right (your WHO) or watching them die.

Our leaders (DI's) did much more than place a rifle in our hands, they taught us how to elevate priorities. With a sense of urgency, they instilled in us the difference between "IN" and "ON" by teaching us "how" to operate our weapons, "why" we needed to master them, and most importantly, "who" it impacted. To better understand the difference between "IN" and "ON" actions in your organization, let's take a quick look at a comparison between the two elements:

IN Actions	ON Actions
Important	Priority
What?/How?	Why?/Who?
Implement	Improve
Effective	Efficient
Tasks	Goals
Train	Develop
Prepare	Plan
Tactical	Strategic
Recruit	Retain
Contact	Sell
Buy	Invest
Decrease Expenses	Increase Profitability

While this list could easily be extended, it will give you a good idea of how to categorize all the elements in your organization – how to fill, and empty, your buckets.

Leadership Link Make the distinction between the "IN" and "ON" actions in your organization, and increase the focus on important tasks, while simultaneously elevating high-priority objectives.

The tasks associated with operating our rifles were important. But focusing on our accuracy was a top priority. While it is probably safe to say that the environment your team works in is not life-threatening, even though some might act like it is, creating a sense of urgency will help you to be more effective at all the "IN" and "ON" elements providing stability and growth.

I have found most leaders have the majority of their time wasted because they are caught up with activities dedicated to working "IN" their organization, or worse yet, those that should be "OUT" of their organization. One of your priority goals will be to consistently dedicate more of your time to the "ON" actions necessary for growth.

As you set *expectations* (Chapter 4) to eliminate the "OUT" actions and *delegate* (Chapter 5) the "IN" actions, you will utilize *accountability* (Chapter 6) to stay on track and position yourself to focus the majority of your time "ON" your priority objectives – making your entire business stronger... greater!

You have probably started to think about the initial reactions from your people. To a disengaged team member, words like expectations, delegation, and accountability are all four-letter words, sounding like nails across a chalkboard. While some people may be resistant at first, you can absolutely take your organization to new levels as you prioritize your actions.

To Elevate Priorities, we must:

- Raise Expectations
- Delegate with a Purpose
- Increase Accountability

Chapter 4

Raise Expectations

Don't Set Low Expectations... You Might Hit Them.

Stepping off the bus at the Recruit Depot was a life-changing experience. Boot camp did not begin with a warm, fuzzy welcome from the Marine Corps. It erupted with yelling, shouting, and an insurmountable amount of confusion. To be clear, the yelling and shouting was the greeting we received from our drill instructors. The confusion was our reaction to this new environment and the Marines who controlled it.

Within the first minute, we were formed up as a platoon. We stood at attention on the infamous yellow footprints painted on the ground, positioned perfectly at a 45-degree angle. As we stood motionless, drill instructors swarmed around us and continued to bark commands, up close and personal, right in our faces.

There was no doubt boot camp would be physically and mentally challenging. As one of the drill instructors stepped up on a platform to address us, this became even more evident. With no uncertainty, he made it clear that not everyone of us would earn the title of U.S. Marine. Although we did not know the exact details of the training we would receive over the next 90 days, one thing was made crystal clear: their expectations. The bar had been raised.

Our drill instructors thoroughly communicated the message that the expectations on our performance were set high; Marine Corps high. Expectations were raised on our physical fitness, our appearance, and our communication. There were also expectations on everything from firing our weapons, and spit-shining our boots, to Marine Corps leadership. By fully understanding the high expectations placed upon us, we were more focused on all of our actions. How focused is your team on their actions?

Leadership Link Unclear expectations lead to conflict.

THE IMPORTANCE OF EXPECTATIONS

I hear people constantly say, "We need to get things prioritized." While it does feel good to say it, it is much better when it actually happens. But most leaders fail to pull it together because they do not properly utilize their *Leadership Bar*. That's right, every leader is issued a bar as soon as they become a leader. Unfortunately, most do not use it for what it was designed for, if they use it at all.

You have one right now. How do you know it's a leadership bar? Because it says "Leadership Bar" on it. How do you know it's yours? Well, that's easy because your name is on it. When you hold onto it, it extends beyond the reach of your two hands. In fact, many hands could fit onto it. And many hands should fit onto it because that is the greatest way to raise the bar in any organization – with your people.

Since every leader must make the decision to lead, a decision must also be made about what to do with your leadership bar. As leaders, we have some options.

Possibilities for your Leadership Bar:

- Set it down and do nothing with it (ignore it)
- Hit people with it (power trip)
- Swipe out the legs from underneath their people (undermine)
- A leader can also lower it (create conflict)

LATIN LESSON

SEMPER PARATUS

Always Ready

Straight from their website, "The Coast Guard is "*Semper Paratus*, 'Always Ready' and we are committed to current and future readiness. We seek the best people, modern technology, resilient infrastructure and capable assets to meet the nation's needs. Every active duty, reserve, civilian and auxiliary member plays an integral role in mission execution."

The Coast Guard is always on the ready as America's maritime first responder, always prepared to defend our coastline. As leaders, we must not only be ready to raise our leadership bars, we must also be prepared to do so with our entire team.

ELIMINATE CONFUSION

When is good not good enough? When great is achievable. But when leaders fail to clarify what is expected, they cannot "expect" to achieve high levels of success. Many leaders assume everyone knows what is expected of them, rather than ensuring that high expectations have been set and communicated throughout their organization.

Leadership Link High expectations lead to unification.

Your team members are not mind readers. Putting them in a position to guess at what your expectations for them are is a guarantee for sub-par performance. Clearly articulating and documenting your expectations will increase performance, which will result in higher morale and results.

Throughout the twelve weeks of basic training, our drill instructors laid out their expectations, with great clarity, before assigning us our tasks. The recruits of Platoon 1095 knew exactly what was expected of us, and by graduation day, our drill instructors had successfully transformed a few, proud recruits into U.S. Marines. What could you do in twelve weeks, when you properly raise the bar?

Most organizations have a significant gap between what the leader expects and what the leader experiences. This gap produces feelings of frustration and discouragement, not only for the leader, but for the team members as well. I have listened to leaders express, in great detail, their annoyance at the lack of their team members' performance. But I have also listened to team members express, in great detail, their annoyance at the lack of clear expectations set by their leaders.

This "expectation" gap will also create confusion and unwanted side effects. Wasted time, poor results, and low morale are only the beginning symptoms of this dilemma. Clearly articulating your expectations might seem like stating the obvious. But you owe it to yourself and to your team members to fill this gap with high expectations, leaving nothing to chance.

When you fail to set high expectations, you leave room for assumptions, doubts, fears, and misunderstandings. You probably noticed I re-emphasized the word *high*. While many leaders fail to set any expectations, others allow low expectations to infect their environment. Would you rather have your team meet high expectations or low expectations? The choice is yours. But so is the responsibility of raising the bar.

I have found many leaders lower their leadership bar because they have a fear of adding stress to their team. If high expectations create stress in a member of your team, you should analyze why that person is in your organization. Low expectations rarely shield anyone from stress. The same team member who feels threatened by high expectations is usually the same person who fails to live up to low expectations. Setting low expectations impacts your organization in three dramatic ways.

The Impact of Low Expectations:

- Protects low performers from higher performance
- Offends high-performance team members
- Establishes you as a low-expectation leader

Lowering your leadership bar is one of the most destructive actions a leader can take. But when leaders convey high expectations to their teams, they create a stronger belief level in their team members' perceptions of their own abilities, the focus of their leaders, and the upward mobility of their organization. If you do not have a strong belief in the abilities of your team, how can they?

In addition, leaders who raise expectations believe in themselves, their role as a leader, and their abilities to guide their teams and achieve results. If you do not believe in yourself, why would your team follow you? The answer is simple. They will not follow you or support you.

Many leaders make a crucial mistake when setting expectations. They only set them for their team members, leaving themselves out of the scenario. For everything, there is a starting point, and for raising expectations, it all begins with the leader.

THE PRINCIPLES OF LEADERSHIP

As a do-it-first, lead-by-example leader, begin by setting high expectations for yourself in your role as a leader. Before you identify what you need to delegate to your team, and how to increase their accountability, clearly articulate what you are responsible for, and what your team can expect from your leadership.

To help enhance perceptions, by clearly defining leadership, we took a closer look at the 14 Leadership Traits of the U.S. Marine Corps. (Chapter 1). These traits have helped to provide the framework for the high levels of leadership that have been synonymous with the Marines since 1775. But Marines are also taught about eleven leadership principles that help to raise the expectations for all Marine leaders.

Just like our military counterparts, every leader wants to raise the bar on performance, but most fail to make an impact when they do not clearly understand the importance of a principle. So, let's take a closer look at the definition of this game-changing word.

principle

noun

- A fundamental **rule**, primary, or general law or truth.
- An accepted or professed **rule** or action or conduct.
- An adopted **rule** or method for application in action.
- A guiding sense of requirements, **rules**, and obligations of right conduct.

It's crystal clear that a principle is also a rule; meant to be followed by leaders – not bent or broken. Once your team understands what they can expect from you, they will deliver on what is expected of them. As you elevate priorities, adopt leadership principles (rules), for the entire team to understand and follow.

Although you will not be marching your troops into life-threatening situations, you do have the ability to lead them into life-changing opportunities by raising expectations with unwavering conviction. Here's a closer look at the leadership principles of the Marine Corps, and how you can translate them into the high expectations needed to improve your performance as a leader.

11 Leadership Principles of the U.S. Marine Corps:

1. **Be Technically and Tactically Proficient** – Maintain a high level of competence in your job skills and leadership skills. Your proficiency will earn the respect of your team as you help them to problem solve, with excellent results. If you cannot understand their job, at the highest levels of excellence, how can you lead them to achieve greater results?

2. **Know Yourself and Seek Self Improvement** – Constantly evaluate your strengths and weaknesses. Improve your weaknesses and utilize your strengths to gain an accurate understanding of yourself, and a keen knowledge of determining the best way to deal with any given situation.

3. **Know Your Marines and Look Out for Their Welfare** – Get to know your team – personally and professionally. This is one of the most important but overlooked principles. Know your team and how they react to different situations. Know them well enough to cast them in the right positions, for their personal growth, and the growth of your organization.

4. **Keep Your Marines Informed** – Providing information can inspire initiative. Informed team members perform better and, if knowledgeable of the situation, can carry on without your direct supervision. Too many leaders fail to keep their team members in the loop, undermining their own efforts. Communicate clearly and often.

5. **Set the Example** – Set the standards for your team by personal example. Your team will observe your appearance, attitude, and performance. With high personal standards, you can expect the same of your team members.

6. **Ensure the Task is Understood, Supervised, and Accomplished** – Before you can expect your team to perform, they need to know what is expected of them. Communicate your instructions in a clear, concise manner, and allow your team a chance to ask questions. Check progress periodically to confirm the assigned task is properly accomplished. *Delegate with a Purpose*, which we will cover in greater detail in Chapter 5.

7. **Train Your Marines as a Team** – Train your team with a purpose and emphasize the essential elements of teamwork. Teach your staff to train, communicate, and operate as a team. Be sure all team members know their positions and responsibilities within the team framework.

8. **Make Sound and Timely Decisions** – Much can be lost when leaders hesitate to make decisions, especially in time-sensitive settings. Improving your internal workflow and raising expectations will allow you to confidently and rapidly assess a situation and make a sound decision. There is no room for reluctance when making important decisions.

9. **Develop a Sense of Responsibility in Your Subordinates** – Delegating important tasks promotes mutual confidence and respect between leaders and team members. Delegating decision-making is the ultimate form of trust and will show your team that you are interested in their personal growth by giving them the opportunity for professional development.

10. **Employ Your Unit in Accordance with its Capabilities** – Successful completion of a task depends upon how well you know your team's capabilities. Seek out challenging tasks for your staff but be sure they are prepared for and have the ability to successfully complete the assignment. Train your team with a purpose.

11. Seek Responsibility and Take Responsibility for Your Actions – Actively seek out challenging assignments for your own professional development and take the responsibility for your actions. You are also responsible for all your team does or fails to do. Be willing to accept justified and constructive criticism. Team members respect leaders who correct their mistakes immediately.

These leadership principles are an essential tool for self-evaluation. By raising expectations for yourself, and seeking constant self-improvement, you can now rightfully set high expectations for your team – you can successfully raise the bar with them.

Leadership Link No matter what challenges you face, leadership is always the solution.

As you elevate priorities, adopt these principles, and they will help guide your actions with yourself and your team, providing a clear example of what is expected of a leader in your organization – what is expected of everyone. As you continue to raise the bar and elevate your entire organization, you will inevitably create additional work (productive work) to remove your OUT's, accomplish your IN's and achieve your ON's.

To do so, it is imperative that you delegate with a purpose.

LEADERSHIP STEPS

RAISE EXPECTATIONS

Elite Leadership Step – IN & ON

- Take a close look at all your actions throughout each day and assess your percentage of time dedicated "Currently" to both IN and ON. Next identify the "Goal" you are shooting for with your time.

	Currently	Goal
IN	_____%	_____%
ON	_____%	_____%

Additional Steps

- **Raise the Bar:** With the support of your team, identify areas you need to see improved, such as communication, attendance, quality, goals, leadership, negative behaviors, turnaround times. Develop a plan to remove your OUT's.

- **IN's:** Make a detailed list of all of your IN's – the important tasks you are responsible for. Many of these will be properly unloaded from your plate through delegation – next chapter.

- **ON's:** Make a list of the priority objectives you would like to dedicate more time to. Your ON's are the actions that will improve your team, department, and organization.

Chapter 5

Delegate with a Purpose

Properly Unload Your Plate.

If you want something done right, do it yourself. How many times have you heard leaders utter this self-defeating statement? They say it to convey the inadequacies of others, but what it ultimately highlights are their short-comings as a leader; their inability to delegate. Leaders who believe they are the only ones capable of doing things right, are incapable of elevating the priorities necessary for growth in their organizations.

When I accepted an entry-level position at the post-production company, I started my first day with the highest expectations for my personal performance. While my position might have been at the bottom of the corporate ladder, my focus was at the top. I quickly mastered the duties and responsibilities of my job description, but I hungered for more.

Before I was in a position to delegate tasks, I requested that more were delegated to me. I assumed responsibility for additional "IN" tasks, so my leaders could focus more of their attention "ON" the priority objectives for the company. Mastering each of my new tasks, I began to help others to become more proficient at their duties. Constantly requesting and mastering the extra assignments delegated to me, resulted in three promotions in eighteen months.

My third promotion was to the position of vice president, and all the leaders in the company now reported directly to me. I reported directly to the owner, and we were well on our way to increasing annual sales by over 300 percent. The process of delegation became one of the most critical disciplines I would embrace as I grew the company, and myself as a leader.

Each promotion presented new opportunities, but also introduced new challenges. My constantly changing job descriptions caused me to transition more and more of my duties to my team. This was not something I took lightly. I knew the tasks I was transitioning to others still played a vital role in supporting the goals of the company, so I made the decision to delegate with a purpose.

Leadership
Link Proper delegation allows leaders to simultaneously empower as they accomplish things through others.

THE IMPORTANCE OF DELEGATION

Delegation is typically in the top five challenges that leaders face. Their reluctance to embrace it is usually due to their inability to define it properly. Let's take a closer look at the definition of this powerful word.

delegate

verb

- To give **control** (responsibility and authority) to someone.
- To **trust** someone with a job, duty, etc.
- To **choose** someone to do something.
- The act of **empowering** to act for another.

For starters, it is a verb. If we travel back to our grade school days, we know that it is an *action* word. Proper delegation does not miraculously happen. Leaders ensure that it occurs – with a purpose.

It is not a shock that, "To give control" is listed. Of course, this is where part of the problem with delegation occurs. When I ask, "How many control freaks do we have here today?" in a room filled with leaders, over half of them quickly raise their hands. Transferring control is a challenging thought. Because most leaders have achieved certain levels of success based on getting things done (taking control), typically their way, it seems counter-intuitive to give that power away.

Leaders are not defined by how much power they have over people. They are defined by how much power they give to people. A leader does not lose power by giving it to someone. On the contrary, they gain more. But transferring control involves high levels of *trust*. We must choose wisely when power exchanges hands.

These are all relevant definitions. But the definition I like the most is the last one, "The act of **empowering**." Nearly every leader agrees that empowering their people is paramount, but few delegate with that purpose in mind. When we properly delegate, we take the first step in empowering our people, which we will cover in greater detail in PART III.

Leadership Delegation is not an option; it is a leadership obligation.
Link

While so much rides on a leader's ability to delegate, so few do it with the end-state in mind – the successful completion of the task. I have found that most delegation is one-sided. Delegation should feel like the smooth transition of the baton from one relay runner to the next. But is is often described as work being "dumped on my plate."

LATIN LESSON

PARI PASSU

Equal Footing

Delegation cannot be a one-sided process. It is imperative that both parties (delegator and delgatee) are on the same page – speaking the same language. There is much more at stake than merely the task. It is critical that everyone steps off together to accomplish each assignment; that everyone has equal footing.

When we go back to Leadership Principle #6, it states that the task (the IN action) should be understood, supervised (it's a team effort), and accomplished. You see, when we delegate, we cannot afford to allow the person to fail. Imagine the impact to their confidence if they fail at a task. Worse yet, imagine the perceptions of the rest of your team when they witness that person failing.

How many of them will want you to delegate something to them? If you allow delegated tasks to fail with your team, you may hear people say, "I'm too *busy*" the next time you try to unload your plate. People should experience the empowering feeling of successfully completing each task, which will encourage everyone to ask for more – to take initiative.

Leaders often ask me, "Why should I develop all of my people as leaders, especially the ones who have no direct reports?" My answer is simple, "Wouldn't you rather delegate a task to someone who has taken the initiative to ask for it, and takes responsibility for their actions, rather than someone waiting to be told to do it?"

Leadership Link Initiative is a critical leadership trait for leaders who want to properly unload their plates.

WHY LEADERS FAIL TO GROW

Tying your children's shoes makes sense when they are three years old. Tying their shoes when they are twenty-three years old, not so much. But it does speak volumes about your parenting skills, or more importantly, your lack of them. When leaders fail to properly transition important duties to their team members, it represents their own leadership limitations.

Far too many leaders are still doing the tasks ("IN's") that they should have properly delegated to their team members long ago. Most leaders have a significant disconnect when it comes to delegation and it prohibits them from focusing "ON" the priority objectives that will elevate their businesses. Some leaders transition responsibilities they should do themselves, while others fail to transition the duties their team members should be doing.

Delegating the important "IN" tasks, necessary for effectively operating your organization, must be done with the highest levels of professionalism. While most leaders acknowledge the importance of delegating important tasks, they often leave out a critical component and their attempts to delegate fall flat.

Properly delegating the task of tying shoes to your child is important but delegating the decision-making ability of choosing the right shoes is more important. When a foot of snow is on the ground, tying a pair of sneakers is not as important as selecting the proper pair of snowshoes.

When we fail to delegate decision-making, in addition to the tasks, we might cause team members to reach an impasse and require far more of our time than we anticipated. When team members ask for additional information to complete a task, it is not uncommon to hear a leader sigh then mumble, "If I want something done right, I'll do it myself."

When transitioning your duties to others, remember to delegate these two critical elements needed for success.

Elements of Delegation:

- Delegate tasks
- Delegate authority

Every leader will agree that delegation is necessary and will free up more time to focus on priority objectives, but most leaders experience little success when they attempt to transition duties to others. Delegating usually turns into nothing more than placing tasks onto someone else's plate, while the leader continues to maintain the decision-making abilities that would allow team members to take initiative and accomplish the task successfully.

It is fair to say that each time a task is delegated, certain variables will arise that will cause a team member to make a decision in order to move the task forward. When the decision-making ability is left out of the delegation, the task will come to a halt. Leaders prohibit growth within their organizations by not properly delegating tasks and decision-making to their team members, simultaneously.

Leadership Link Delegate the authority to make the decisions necessary for success.

With so much riding on the successful delegation of important tasks, you cannot afford to leave anything to chance. In order to focus the majority of your efforts "ON" the priority objectives that will enhance your organization, you must accomplish many things through the efforts of others. The effective use of time, resources, and people will allow the leader, the team, and the company to grow simultaneously.

DELEGATE WITH A PURPOSE – O.D.S.

One of the most common leadership topics I am requested to train on is delegation. Focused on achieving greater results, many leaders become frustrated at their inability to relinquish even the most basic tasks. Their desire to ensure that everything is completed correctly, matched with their ineffectiveness as a delegator, results in the perception that they are "control freaks" or "micro-managers."

With important tasks piling up on their plates, most leaders are often too busy handling the "IN" items to be able to focus "ON" the items necessary for growth. When I share the benefits of delegation with leaders, I am always met with nods of approval. To transform the *delegation disconnect*, into a leadership connection, I introduce a new delegation system.

As the vice president of a corporation that was experiencing exponential growth, delegation was one of my keys to success. It was also the key to our high-level results. In order to delegate all the tasks and decision-making necessary, I developed a process that would leave nothing to chance. I found that delegation worked best when it was applied with detailed orchestration and direct supervision. To delegate with a purpose, always focus on the O.D.S. principle for success.

Delegate with a Purpose – O.D.S.:

- **O**rchestrate
- **D**elegate
- **S**upervise

Orchestrate

Consider all the possible variables in any given assignment you are delegating. If something can go wrong, it probably will. This is precisely why you need to identify any decision-making duties that will support the completion of the task.

Orchestration is more than coordination. It is the creation of the blueprints for success, combining three crucial steps.

To Orchestrate: Plan – Train – Allocate

Having a clear plan for the successful completion of each task will allow you to communicate the high expectations you have for its completion. Your plan must include the procedures, the variables, and the solutions needed for positive results.

As you develop the details of your plan, factor in any necessary training needed, prior to delegating the task. While some leaders have every detail coordinated, they fail to train the team member responsible for the task, setting the person up for failure from the outset.

Processes that seem simple and straightforward to the leader might not be so easy for someone who has never encountered them before. Too many leaders assign tasks to people who are not properly trained, and this ultimately results in frustration and resentment for everyone.

Be patient and realize that training also requires you to listen to their questions and concerns. It should go without saying that the orchestration phase is the best time to hear their thoughts. Unfortunately, many leaders wait until the task has already been delegated. You should always anticipate questions. Deciding which phase this happens in is up to you.

Training is a long-term investment in your delegation system. Be mindful that the time spent in the training process will significantly minimize the time spent correcting mistakes.

The last component of the orchestration phase is to allocate all the resources required to complete the task. Forms and documents, passwords and equipment need to be readily available to allow timelines to be met. If you do not orchestrate effectively, you will pay the price later.

Leadership Link Leaders empower people by delegating control, not holding onto it.

Delegate

Detailed orchestration makes the delegation phase simple and effective. Having invested the necessary time in planning, training, and allocating resources, your communication will be clear, concise, and well-received by everyone involved in the assignment. The negative perception of "dumping" projects will soon transform into a results-oriented transition of tasks and decision-making.

During this phase, provide any additional clarification about the task and the authority needed, and allow your team members the opportunity to ask any additional questions. To boost the confidence of your staff, reemphasize the support they can expect from you and anyone else involved with this task.

Offering the proper support is the key to not becoming the dreaded "micro-manager." I have always found it beneficial to articulate how I successfully accomplished the task, while leaving room for the individual to do it in ways that work best for them. Focus more on the results and less on the formality of the procedure. When you treat someone like a person who is capable of taking initiative, they will typically be inclined to take it more often.

Supervise

Now that you have delegated the task you so diligently orchestrated, you will need to regularly connect with your team about their progress. Supervising is about course-correcting. Set up meetings, as needed, to discuss strengths and weaknesses. Allow your team to communicate their challenges and offer constructive feedback for their development. This is the time to help them problem-solve. Guiding them through their failures will build trust and confidence.

Each phase should require less of your time, but more of your direct input.

PROPER DELEGATION EMPOWERS

When you delegate with a purpose, you are making a significant investment. It might seem like delegation will initially slow you down, but in the long run, it will increase productivity exponentially and allow you to further elevate priorities.

Everything we did in the Marine Corps, even the tasks we despised, such as qualifying in the gas chamber, served a greater purpose. Our first encounter with this chemical-warfare testing ground occurred in boot camp. Each recruit spent approximately 3-5 minutes, perhaps the longest 3-5 minutes of our lives, in a chamber filled with chlorobenzylidene malononitrile, commonly referred to as CS Gas.

Typically used as a riot control agent, we were trained how to properly wear our masks in this environment. But the true test came when we were ordered to remove our masks. As the gas swirled around our faces, we held our breath and kept our eyes tightly closed. As we were instructed to "don and clear," we quickly placed our masks back on, covered our filters, and exhaled to blow any gas out of our masks. We slowly opened our eyes and cautiously inhaled a small breath of air. Success! There was no gas in our masks.

Unfortunately, that was only the first part of being qualified. The next step was not as pleasant. We needed to experience the gas, without our masks. One by one, we stepped up to our drill instructors. We were ordered to remove our masks and open our eyes. Holding my breath, I opened my eyes and they quickly felt the searing sting of the gas. To assist me in taking a breath, I was instructed to recite my general orders. I made it to number three when my lungs begged for air – a moment I will never forget.

My eyes were pouring tears from the unbearable burning sensation and my lungs immediately shut down as they filled with gas. I could no longer breathe. It felt like I was dying. As I hurried out of the tent and into fresh air, I realized the greater purpose of this task – to stay alive. Learning how to operate in a hostile environment was critical and our drill instructors had a deep level of buy-in from every member of Platoon 1095.

In addition to conveying the *purpose* of our assignment, our DI's *orchestrated* every variable involved with this task. They *delegated* the actions to us, complete with the training necessary for success. Leaving nothing to chance, they *supervised* our efforts and provided their guidance throughout the entire process – they were in the tent with us. After surviving the gas chamber, we not only felt relieved, we felt empowered.

THE RULE OF THREE

Whether we are assigning goals or delegating tasks to our team members, it is imperative to make sure they are not feeling overwhelmed. Too many leaders delegate too much at once. One of the most important concepts I learned in the Marine Corps was *The Rule of Three.*

INC. Magazine did an article on the Corps and stated, "The rule dictates that a person should limit his or her attention to three tasks or goals. When applied to strategizing, the rule prescribes boiling a world of infinite possibilities down to three alternative courses of action. Anything more and a Marine can become overextended and confused. The Marines experimented with a rule of four and found that effectiveness plummeted."

Leadership Link Limit delegated tasks to three to increase effectiveness and success.

THE RULE OF THIRDS – D.S.O.

If you have ever taught a teenage how to drive, you understand proper delegation. If a parent "dumps" the keys into their child's hand, allows them to go out and drive by themselves, and merely hopes for the best, it is fair to say that may be described as bad parenting. When a leader "dumps" a task on a team member, allows them to go at it alone, and merely hopes for the best, it is fair to say that may be described as bad leadership.

When I ask parents their techniques for teaching a teenager to drive, they share the same three steps.

1. Start in an empty parking lot

2. Move on to side streets

3. Advance to the freeway

Following the right steps is critical when delegating. Imagine how a teenager would feel if you had them start with the freeway. Also, where is the parent during all of this? Right there in the passenger seat. They are available to help guide and course-correct. Just like learning to drive, a delegated task can be an exciting and anxious time. The Rule of Thirds allows you to transition tasks seamlessly.

One of the most important tasks I had at the media company was hiring. I had it down to a science and performed it at the highest levels. I had been bringing people into our company for a long time, but as we grew, I knew I needed to delegate this to our leaders.

This was the lifeblood of our culture, so there was a lot at stake. I needed it to be a successful transition and so did our leaders. Using the Rule of Thirds, I broke the transition into three parts that allowed success and empowerment to occur.

The Rule of Thirds – D.S.O.:

- **D**eliver
- **S**hare
- **O**bserve

It is not uncommon for leaders to neglect delegation by saying, "It's faster to do it myself." While temporarily true, it permanently robs the team of their empowerment and traps leaders "IN" the business. A new way of looking at delegation is to understand that you are going to do the tasks anyways, so it makes sense to pull someone in and train them, using *The Rule of Thirds*. Because I typically interviewed about 10 people for each position, I decided to schedule nine interviews (easier math) and employ *The Rule of Thirds*.

Deliver

I *delivered* the first three interviews. The team member I was training was not required to say anything – merely *observe*. There was no pressure. After each interview we discussed areas they felt confident that they could *deliver*.

Share

We *shared* the next three interviews, based on their level of comfort. I could also step in, as needed, to guide and course-correct. After each interview we discussed more of the areas they felt confident in *delivering*.

Observe

I *observed* each team member as they *delivered* these three interviews. I was there to offer support, if needed.

Typically, by the ninth interview, they completely had it and were saying things better than I did. They were confident, excited, and empowered. After all, isn't that why we hire and build people, to be better than us? It would be foolish to hire and build people to be worse.

Delegating with a purpose takes an investment on your part but pays you back in more ways than you can ever calculate. Now that you have learned how to delegate with a purpose, it is time to further elevate priorities as you *Increase Accountability*.

LEADERSHIP STEPS

DELEGATE WITH A PURPOSE

Elite Leadership Step – Rule of Three

- Delegation begins with your list of "IN's" (important tasks - from the Leadership Steps at the end of Chapter 4). Identify:

  o Three important **tasks** that need to be delegated off your plate

  o The **team members** who will take over these responsibilities

  o The level of **authority** they need to be successful

Additional Steps

- **Purpose:** Get off-site with each of the team members you selected to share the purpose behind the important task that you will be delegating to them. Go over the steps in **O.D.S.** to build their confidence – and yours.

- **Rule of Thirds:** With each team member, use the *Rule of Thirds* to help schedule their days, including your involvement (supervision) as they take the "IN's" off of your plate (with purpose).

- **Your Schedule:** As you successfully delegate some of your "IN's", you will buy back time to work "ON" your business. Schedule your "Golden Time," the blocks of uninterrupted time to work on your *priority objectives.*

Chapter 6

Increase Accountability

Tracking Your Way to a Partnership.

"When am I going to get those reports?" "When is that thing going to be finished?" "Who dropped the ball on that order?" "Who's responsible for that?" Does any of this sound familiar? In most organizations, leaders ask these types of questions more than they should, often receiving the same answer, "I don't know, it's not my job!"

Without a doubt, it is important to know who is responsible. But an even more crucial question should be, "How can we improve?" Without the proper accountability in place, leaders and team members will encounter more frustration and less trust. When the workplace lacks accountability, it misses out on opportunities for growth, most of which are in plain sight.

As you *Set High Expectations* and *Delegate with a Purpose*, you must also *Increase Accountability*. Raising the bar on personal responsibility throughout your organization, by providing a standard expectation of accountability everyone clearly understands, will allow you to further *Elevate Priorities*. Failure to implement accountability will result in the blame game.

Leadership Link Accountability removes the fog clouding your team's vision.

Tactical solutions will be replaced by finger pointing, creating a negative impact on you, your team, and your customers. Without accountability, the path to sustainable growth is nearly invisible. Accountability will help your organization to increase productivity and team morale, while simultaneously improving customer satisfaction. While it will bring great results, many leaders struggle with the implementation and maintenance of this powerful tactic.

THE IMPORTANCE OF ACCOUNTABILITY

Is there a difference between leading and managing? Most people readily agree that there is but struggle to identify what differentiates each word. In its most simple form, I believe that we need to manage the work and lead the people. Manage budgets, inventory, shift schedules, and processes.

But lead the people. Encourage them, inspire them, empower them. Guide them, coach them, mentor them. Because many leaders "manage" their people, *accountability* often loses it full impact and is thought of as nothing more than "micro-management." It is not uncommon for people to perceive accountability as, "My boss is just checking up on me."

LATIN LESSON

EXCELLENTIA per SOCIETATEM

Excellence through Partnership

Accountability, in its purest form is a partnership between people. It takes leaders of great character to not only hold people accountable but to be accountable themselves. When you increase accountability and some people leave, they are typically the "busy" people, not your productive team members. The benefits of accountability will always outweigh the lack of accountability.

Let's take a closer look at the definition of this word to develop a deeper understanding of its significance.

accountability

noun

- The quality or state of being **responsible**.
- An obligation or willingness to accept **responsibility**.
- The state of being accountable, liable, answerable or **responsible**.
- Expected to be **responsible** for one's actions.

It is evident that the act of being accountable is a direct link to greater levels of responsibility. Now to really blow your minds, let's revisit two critical leadership principles:

#9 - Develop a sense of **responsibility** in your subordinates (the people).

#11 - Seek **responsibility** and take **responsibility** for your actions (the leader).

In the eleven leadership principles of the United States Marnie Corps, the word *responsibility* is mentioned three times. How important is it to the Corps? How seriously do they take accountability? Do not let this word be a source of contention in your organization. Fulfill your purpose as a leader and create a partnership through accountability.

Leadership Link Accountability is the manifestation of an ownership mindset in each team member.

Imagine, just for a moment, what your culture would feel like if every person on your team took responsibility for their actions. What would it feel like as everyone embraces accountability and perceives it as a partnership, a way of keeping each other informed and making the course-corrections necessary for success? While there are many benefits of increasing accountability, here are the top five.

The Benefits of Accountability:

- Accelerates Performance

- Increases Engagement

- Provides Insights

- Identifies Key Players

- Re-establishes Purpose

When accountability is increased and you have continued to develop everyone as leaders, you will soon begin to achieve a long-lost treasure: *Voluntary Accountability*. This is when team members proactively keep their leaders and their team members informed. Remember, leadership principle #4 – Keep Your Marines Informed.

THE OBSTACLES OF ACCOUNTABILITY

With the hopes of stellar performance, leaders often dream about the results they will see as their team members voluntarily and enthusiastically assume high levels of personal responsibility. Think about it for a moment – commitments upheld, rules being followed, tough decisions being resolved, sales numbers up, and expenses down.

This dream scenario is usually short-lived. Once awake, the obstacles of accountability create stress and frustration for leaders at all levels within an organization. Those who believe in the positive benefits of accountability often struggle to successfully implement it within their teams. Accountability is typically perceived with great pessimism by most employees, associating it with negativity, discipline, and punishment.

Unfortunately, these dismal perceptions are accurate, rooted deeply in the failures of other leaders. When a leader lacks the dedication and commitment necessary to eliminate the three obstacles of accountability, their organization suffers. Standards begin to slip, and people fail to perform up to their true potential.

3 Obstacles of Accountability:

1. Lack of Action

2. Focus on Poor Performance

3. Failure to Recognize Achievement

Lack of Action

Accountability is not taken seriously because it typically receives more lip service than action. Most leaders use reports to show team members that they are aware of their efforts but offer little-to-no constructive recommendations on how to improve their performance. Some leaders track too little, while others track too much. Regardless of the quantity, a common frustration among team members is that nothing is done positively with the information collected.

Unacknowledged accountability is despised by everyone. When someone takes the time, puts in the effort, and uses resources to provide a leader with an accountability report, some form of action is expected. To do or say nothing about it results in discouragement. Ultimately, you will begin to receive the bare minimums of what you are requesting.

Leadership Link Only track something that you are prepared to take action on.

Focus on Poor Performance

In most organizations, accountability is set in motion for the wrong reason – to simply fix a negative situation. "Too many people are late to work, so we'll track their attendance." "Sales are down, so let's focus on their contacting efforts." "Expenses are too high, so we need to monitor their spending." Leaders who step in only when something is wrong are perceived as the bearers of bad news, and team members become uneasy in their presence.

After a series of intense meetings, warnings, and write-ups, performance might briefly improve, causing the focus on accountability to decrease. As the performance begins to dip again, accountability is again raised. This negative cycle causes a temporary change in patterns, but not the permanent enhancements in behavior required to achieve greater results.

Leadership Link Use the power of tracking to end the cycles of poor performance.

Failure to Recognize Achievement

Leaders tend to focus their time and efforts on fixing the negative performance of their low-performing team members, rather than recognizing the positive performance of their star players. Over time, a lack of accountability will cause deep resentment in those who have provided outstanding performance. When more attention is dedicated to poor performance rather than top-tier achievement, these team members will seek organizations that embrace accountability and reward excellent performance.

Conversely, the organizations lacking accountability struggle to attract top talent because those types of professionals need to be in an environment that values their positive attributes of accountability.

As you eliminate the *Three Obstacles of Accountability*, you will deliver more recognition for high performance, and dedicate less time reprimanding low performance. Accountability is much more than receiving a spread sheet with some numbers. It is a partnership for success and for building a better organization.

LEADERSHIP TOOLS

In Ethiopia, the earliest findings show that man learned the importance of creating and enhancing tools approximately 2.6 million years ago. Specialized stone tools, used for hammering, fighting, hunting and butchering animals, were not just stumbled upon, they were manufactured. They were designed to support a priority goal: survival.

Even chimpanzees understand the benefit of using basic tools to hunt their prey and forage for ants. But it is the extent to which humans have developed and utilized tools that makes it one of the greatest factors that separates us from animals. What separates you from other leaders? What tools are you using to improve the results of your team, your results as a leader, and the results of your organization?

Leaders are builders. Successful leaders build team members, new leaders, and strong organizations. It is detrimental to your success to do it without the use of tools, which help to collapse time frames, allowing for greater precision, and ultimately producing greater results.

The failure of accountability can be directly linked to the ineffective use, or complete disregard, of the leadership tools necessary to raise the bar on performance and achieve greater results. After all, isn't that what accountability should be focused on: performance and results? Using the following leadership tools, will allow you to create a system for increasing accountability.

Leadership Tools for Increasing Accountability:

- Flight Plan
- Organizational Charts
- Job Descriptions
- Workflow
- Evaluations

Before we take a closer look at the vital importance of each tool, understand that most of the leaders who I encounter have tried, unsuccessfully, to build their team and their organization without using leadership tools. They strive for greater results but leave the required tools untouched in their toolboxes.

When I ask for the current version of these tools, I typically get a response such as, "Um... hold on for a second... you know, actually we're still updating our plan" or "Our job descriptions are here somewhere." Yes, it is difficult to use a hammer if it is still being manufactured.

Most organizations have some version of these tools, but merely check them off a list as "completed." When leaders fail to take them out of their toolbox and use them for their true purpose, they fail to effectively increase accountability. Separate yourself from other leaders by strengthening, implementing, and utilizing these powerful tools.

Flight Plan

The priority goals you identified in Chapter 3 were never meant to be tucked away. These goals are the focal point of your Flight Plan (Chapter 10) and the driving force for accountability. They provide clarity and certainty. Everything your organization does should support the accomplishment of your plan.

Priority goals magnify the passion needed to create high levels of accountability, while providing the team with direction and clarity. Increasing accountability is not about providing the leader with information, it is about analyzing key data and course-correcting to ensure that your plan is on track and the goals are not only met but exceeded. Regularly discuss your plan and the goals of your organization, especially as it relates to all forms of accountability.

Organizational Charts

Just as a sports coach draws the "X's" and "O's" on a play chart, leaders must position their team members for the big win. Organizational charts are rarely visible in most organizations, but they are the first link to successfully accomplish the goals in your Flight Plan.

More than assigning a name to a job, your organizational chart identifies the positions and people necessary to support the accomplishment of all key objectives. Every position should serve a purpose, and every person should play an important role in the success of your plan.

Accountability will help to identify the positions needed, and those no longer required. As your organizational chart evolves to meet the needs of your goals, it will provide a snapshot of the current and future team required for success.

In just one year, the organizational chart that I created, changed three times; eliminating, adding, and enhancing the positions necessary to support our current and future growth. The next version of your Organizational Chart is your *Opportunity Chart*, detailing the new positions (opportunities) coming from your growth.

Leadership Link Begin to track the elements that will provide opportunities for recognition.

Job Descriptions

People struggle to be accountable when the expectations from their leaders are not clearly defined and written down. When job descriptions are used, many leaders hand them out with a stack of other documents to be reviewed by the team member, not used as a tool to outline the high expectations for their performance.

It is hard to hold anyone accountable when there is ambiguity with their role. This leads to confusion and a lack of initiative. Job descriptions are powerful tools for accountability and open the line of communication with everyone. Each word on that form should have a definitive purpose.

When creating job descriptions, include the following:

Overview   how this role supports the plan (purpose)

Duties   responsibilities of each team member (accountability)

Requirements   the skills required for success (training)

Signatures   the team member and the leader sign the form (partnership)

By having both the leader and the team member sign this tool, each person will be responsible for ensuring that the team member is technically and tactically proficient at the required elements for the position. Job descriptions should constantly be reviewed as they highlight key areas of training needed to get that person fully qualified to perform those duties.

Workflow

Every company has specific policies and procedures for "how" things need to be done properly. If they do not, they need them. Workflow is the process of enhancing efficiencies and eliminating mistakes, showing those "who" are responsible for doing something, "how" to do it properly.

Whether your team processes orders, ships materials, or submits forms internally, a detailed workflow will allow the work to transition from start to finish, with the least amount of resistance and mistakes. Once designed, workflow can be easily modified to accommodate new products, services, regulations, etc.

In the media business, with the support of my leadership team, we invested our time and resources to create a workflow system that helped reduce our outgoing error ratio from 15% to .35%. Yes, almost one-third of one percent. Our workflow increased the number of people checking the status of each order, and it significantly decreased our error ratio, even as we grew.

Our improvements resulted in less mistakes and more satisfied customers. Our team could fulfill the expectations in their job descriptions and our customers could count on us for outstanding results. Develop a workflow that will allow everyone to do their jobs with the highest possibility for success. For many leaders, the perfect workflow exists in their heads. Taking the time necessary to show the proper protocols to your team will eliminate the, "If I want something done right..." dialogue.

Evaluations

Too many leaders miss out on the amazing opportunities they have to provide guidance, coaching, and positive course-correcting. They neglect to set regular performance evaluations, leaving the personal and professional development of their team members to their own vices. How well do you think that works?

Leaders often mistake intent for performance, not realizing that their team members have a strong desire for improvement. By having solid job descriptions, as well as an effective workflow system, you are armed to provide the necessary feedback for success. As you discuss the duties and responsibilities you both have signed off on, you will open honest dialogue for improvement. You might also hear powerful suggestions on how to make things even better.

Accountability allows leaders to gain valuable insights and discover new opportunities for growth. It also identifies the necessary positions and the team members needed to get the job done.

Leadership Link Conduct evaluations regularly, searching for areas of improvement and identifying opportunities to recognize great performance.

Accountability allows you to *Elevate Priorities*, but it also helps to strengthen your ability to *Empower People*.

LEADERSHIP STEPS

INCREASE ACCOUNTABILITY

Elite Leadership Step – Assess Your Accountability Tools

- Assess how effective the following accountability tools are being used in your organization, using a scale of 1-10 (10 being best).

  - Flight Plan   _____

  - Organizational Charts   _____

  - Job Descriptions   _____

  - Workflow   _____

  - Evaluations   _____

Additional Steps

- **Current:** Make a list of all forms of accountability being used: sales reports, inventory lists, etc. How can they be enhanced/used better?

- **Future:** What forms of accountability are needed to grow your organization and keep it on track?

- **Recognition:** Because accountability allows us to track performance, determine the necessary recognition plan to reward and incentivize those performing above par, while encouraging everyone to embrace accountability.

Part III

Empower People

Part III

Empower People

Move from Ready to Prepared.

I let out a huge sigh of relief as I clicked "Save," signaling that the final touches on our infrastructure had been completed. All of our t's were crossed and our i's were dotted. It was a major undertaking, but overhauling our policies and procedures helped us to outline everything our team needed in order to be ready for the high levels of growth we were projecting.

Our organizational chart depicted the necessary team structure, while our job descriptions detailed the duties and responsibilities of each team member. By improving our sales system and upgrading our operational workflow, we further increased our ability to succeed. Everyone knew what was expected and we were excited to pursue the goals necessary to take our company to the next level. But one question lingered in the back of my mind. Were our people empowered enough to make it through any upcoming challenges and potential set-backs?

THE IMPORTANCE OF EMPOWERMENT

I knew the dramatic difference between being ready – and being prepared. Flashing back to 1987 again, I remember the intense training I received as a young Marine. Attached to every task and objective were the highest levels of excellence. Being proficient in my job duties as an air traffic controller, and qualifying as a sharp shooter with my rifle, made me feel ready for anything. But the Marine Corps never settles on only being ready.

August 2, 1990 was the day before my 21st birthday. It was also the same day the world watched as Iraq invaded Kuwait. On that day, the United States prepared for war. As Operation Desert Storm drew closer, I remember my thoughts shifting from how ready I was; to how prepared was I? My service in the Corps had covered three years, but all during peace time. Everything intensified on that day as we headed toward the rising conflict in the Middle East.

Our leaders ensured that we were ready for deployment by supplying us with all of the necessary gear. From head to toe, we carried nearly 80 pounds of equipment. Loaded with helmets, flak jackets, ammunition, and canteens, we strapped on our back packs, which were filled with the additional gear necessary for life in the field.

Our orders, the "policies and procedures" we would be following, were communicated to us in great detail. Every Marine clearly understood the mission. The objectives that were necessary to accomplish our goals were of the highest priority. We were ready. But in the brief time leading up to our deployment, our leaders ensured that we were also prepared. They focused on the highest levels of teamwork.

Providing us with much more than supplies and orders, we were empowered with the ability to take ownership of our situation; to take the initiative needed to succeed. On my 21st birthday, our training immediately commenced in the excruciating heat of the Yuma desert.

Wearing full combat gear, we marched through the sandy terrain, which resembled the harsh Saudi Arabian environment where we would soon be deployed. As we continued to move forward, under the unrelenting temperatures, our leaders presented us with challenges to sharpen our skills. They provided every opportunity possible to empower us, not all of which were pleasant.

Through the blistering heat, often breaking 115 degrees, gas canisters were launched in our direction, simulating a chemical attack by the enemy. Having our masks made us ready but being able to effectively use them under extreme conditions and circumstances helped us to be prepared. But what if a fellow Marine was not able to put on his mask fast enough? We were empowered to think on our feet.

Each Marine was issued 2 PAM Chloride, a nerve agent treatment. Using autoinjector devices, we could effectively administer this life-saving chemical to ourselves, or a fellow Marine. Thrusting the injector into the outer thigh muscle, a powerful dose would be released from the needle and into the bloodstream.

As new challenges were introduced, the Marines in my unit faced them with the highest levels of professionalism and resolve. Our leaders empowered us with the ability to act as a team and employ fast-acting, life-saving decisions without having to wait for the order to do so. How do your people currently handle challenges? Are they handling them the way you desire?

While my father's poor health prevented me from being deployed, my unit was sent to Saudi Arabia to support Operation Desert Storm. The Marines in my platoon were not only ready for the difficult circumstances ahead, they were prepared for a successful campaign. We were not trained to perform as a group of a Marines; we were developed to act as a team. There is a significant difference between a group and a team.

Leadership Link Leaders are committed to creating a team of leaders who foster synergy.

GROUP VS. TEAM

Most leaders only experience true teamwork by reading about it, not by working with an actual team. There is no doubt that a team can accomplish amazing things, but far too many leaders hand out the title of "Team" too quickly. When you walk into the office, do you work with a *group* of employees or a *team* of leaders?

Neither distinction means that you have bad people, it just describes how they perform together. When I give presentations on team-building, I show two different pictures of dogs. The top picture shows 8 happy puppies. The bottom picture features 8 sled dogs - Alaskan Malamutes. I ask, "Which is the picture of a team?" and everyone immediately yells out, "The bottom picture." They are correct.

It's interesting that we can easily distinguish between a group of dogs and a team of dogs, but sometimes struggle to have such clarity with the people we work with. There is nothing wrong with puppies. They are typically excited to see you and enthusiastic about everything. But what might happen if you toss a big meaty bone in the middle of these puppies? They may turn on each other. Again, that does not make them bad dogs.

But to go somewhere, you need an empowered team. Whether you are crossing the frozen tundra or striving to build a greater business, a team will always serve you best. People who perform like a group are not necessarily bad people either. They are just not delivering what empowered team members are capable of. To fully understand the difference between a group and a team, let's look at the three characteristics of each.

The Three Key Characteristics of a:

GROUP	**TEAM**
Acts as **individuals**	Acts as a **cohesive unit**
Focuses on **personal objectives**	Focuses on **common objectives**
Performs in the **moment**	Performs for the **future**

EMPOWERING YOUR TEAM

The level of training I received in the Marine Corps showed me the difference between being ready and being prepared. It also emphasized the need for leaders to channel their energy into empowering people. As an executive corporate leader, focused on growth, my ability to empower people would become a determining factor in achieving greater results.

At the post-production company, I had enhanced perceptions (Part 1) and elevated priorities (Part 2), but I knew our success would not be achieved if I failed to empower the people in our organization. I was determined to replace the old way of thinking with a new environment of innovation; one that allowed our people to transform from "do-what-I-have-to-do" workers to "out-of-the-box" performers.

Leadership Link When we empower people, we create an environment that is more conducive for building teams of leaders (everyone is a leader).

Most leaders are shocked at the lack of action their team members actually take. Perhaps they still believe that *knowledge creates action*. It does not. But I have found a simple formula that will get team members moving in the right direction:

KNOWLEDGE does not create ACTION.

EMPOWERMENT creates ACTION.

ACTION enhances KNOWLEDGE.

Both empowered and non-empowered people have specific dialogue that you can hear. When leaders present new opportunities for growth to their teams, they are often met with, "Here's why we can't do it." To achieve sustainable upward momentum, leaders need empowered team members who choose the option, "Here's how we can do it."

Imagine walking into your office and being surrounded by a team of people who take ownership of their duties and responsibilities. Think about the benefits of having team members who focus their efforts on finding solutions and creating opportunities, rather than identifying problems and settling for average.

Most leaders would do anything possible to have a team of proactive, empowered people who can function as both a cohesive unit and succeed autonomously. But the problem is they do not do everything necessary to have a team like this. The leader is often the root of the problem, inadvertently creating a lackluster mindset in their organization, rather than a culture of empowerment.

Leaders ignore empowerment because they do not truly understand it. It is not assigning a task to be completed; that is achieved by proper delegation. Empowerment is not providing instructions, nor is it leaving someone to their own devices. Neither is it micro-management. Empowerment is about helping your team to achieve personal growth and certainty. It is about presenting them with opportunities to think for themselves, and to make decisions confidently.

When you empower people, you give them the authorization to take initiative, to be creative, and to become independent. When you empower people, you transform them from reactive to proactive. After all, doesn't every leader want a proactive team?

Leadership Link When you empower people, you allow them to unleash their full potential, positioning your organization for new levels of success.

When the people are empowered, the environment promotes creativity. As team members take more initiative, they will find new solutions they might have missed had they adhered to rigid guidelines. Leaders who recognize their people for their ideas, will instill a sense of pride and accomplishment, encouraging further initiative. Empowering your people will break them out of the traditional boss-employee mindset, and will build trust, self-confidence, achievement, and teamwork.

But if it were easy to empower people, every leader would do it. Leaders must ensure that their environment encourages team members to take initiative, rewarding them for taking action without being asked. This can be fostered by linking together the elements that allow empowerment to flow!

- Communication
- Cultivation
- Collaboration

Chapter 7

Communication

Getting Everyone to Speak the Same Language.

Learning to focus on enunciation and vocabulary, grammar and punctuation, we are taught an understanding of our language from our earliest days of school. But the skills needed to properly speak and write do not qualify us to speak "leadership" and lead people, much less empower them. To make the leadership connection with communication, more than an academic approach is necessary.

The communication styles of most leaders vary significantly.

- Some can be passive while others take a more aggressive approach.
- Some use elements of manipulation while others choose motivation.
- Leaders can be assertive, direct, and crystal-clear.
- They can also be vague, indirect, and misleading.

Regardless of their style, each leader sends a message every time they communicate. This message reaffirms their strengths and weaknesses – their conviction to the greater purpose of the organization, and their ability to successfully guide their team to the desired destination. A leader's message must be a consistent, positive, reassurance about their intent.

THE IMPORTANCE OF COMMUNICATION

Because every word, every gesture, and every action sends a powerful message, even the smallest form of communication has the ability to make a significant impact. When leaders are not aware of their communication style, they may fail to make the impact they intend. We must pay particular attention to each part. A little goes a long way.

LATIN LESSON

MULTUM in PARVO

Much in Little

To measure the effectiveness of a message being sent, leaders can rank their level of communication by using three categories. Identifying the type of communication used in your organization will allow you to make the adjustments necessary to transform it into a tool of empowerment.

3 Levels of Communication:

1. Poor

2. Basic

3. Dynamic

Leaders can typically trace organizational problems, issues, and challenges back to poor communication. When dialogue fails to deliver the appropriate message, companies experience significantly more damage than the initial mistakes caused only by misunderstandings.

Leadership Link Use C.P.C. to regularly connect with people – Constant Personal Communication.

POOR COMMUNICATION

Poor communication will erode a leader's ability to enhance perceptions, elevate priorities, and empower people. When those three leadership purposes suffer, it will be nearly impossible to achieve our fourth purpose – exceed expectations. No matter how minor, the impact of poor communication can have major effects.

The Impact of Poor Communication:

- Destroys morale
- Minimizes effectiveness
- Discourages innovation
- Reduces efficiencies
- Eliminates collaboration

Poor communication often occurs when leaders use it as a device to simply transition information from one person to the next, but leave communication gaps, filled with doubt, misunderstandings, and a lack of trust. By failing to attach a distinct purpose to their dialogue, their ambiguity inadvertently leaves room for unintended interpretations of their comments.

Examples of Poor Communication

- Negative dialogue
- Derogatory comments
- Incomplete communication
- Late communication
- Lack of clarity
- Too much information
- Lack of follow-up
- Unanswered communication

Leadership Link Poor communication is one of the first OUT's to remove from your organization.

BASIC COMMUNICATION

Awareness of poor communication is the first step. The next step, toward the creation of an environment that fosters a high level of empowerment, is developing a mastery of basic communication skills. I have yet to meet a leader who set out to be a poor communicator. Most leaders do not plan to fall short in this important arena. But when knowledge of basic communication skills is absent, only sub-par results can be achieved.

Leaders who are reluctant to embrace basic communication skills, will magnify the barriers preventing their message from reaching their audience. Both physical and psychological barriers can create a filtering effect and lessen the impact of a leader's message. Communication barriers such as stress, culture, noise, and perception can filter out important components of a leader's dialogue.

Great communicators develop a keen external awareness of any obstacles to communication and put forth great efforts to minimize their impact by maximizing their basic communication skills. Involving much more than merely coordinating dialogue, leaders must ensure that their message is able to pass through any barrier existing between them and their audience. Effective communicators develop an understanding of the three elements of basic communication.

The 3 Elements of Basic Communication:

1. Words

2. Body Language

3. Actions

Words

Words are the invisible tools that can influence thoughts and behaviors. In addition to choosing the appropriate words to convey a message, leaders should pay attention to the tone of their voices. Certainty and conviction will be translated more by the inflections of the voice, than by the actual spoken words.

Leadership Link Choose your words wisely and deliver them with passion.

Body Language

Every gesture, from hand movements and eye contact, to facial expressions and body posture, signals the audience about the true nature of the leader's intentions. While people are listening to a leader speak, they are watching every move intently to develop a deeper understanding of the meaning behind the message. A simple sigh or eyeroll, from a leader, can make a significant impact, but unfortunately a negative one.

Leadership Link Be aware of your verbal and non-verbal communication.

Actions

A powerful message will inspire immediate action from the audience. But the actions of the leader deliver the most compelling message of all. Leaders' actions emulate their belief level in their own message. What a leader does when people are not around is equally as important as what is done when they are around.

Leadership Link One bad action will undermine a thousand great words.

CORPS COMMUNICATION

You could hear a pin drop as the bus door swung open. Calculated and meticulous, a Marine Corps drill instructor stepped in, turned, and faced us. Still wearing our civilian clothes, we sat there in silence, but not for long. With an explosion of dynamic communication, and colorful words I cannot write in this book, the chiseled sergeant communicated that we needed to quickly exit that bus. Within seconds, each seat was empty.

Boot camp had officially begun. Over the next ninety days, the communication we experienced from our drill instructors was much more than barking orders, screaming instructions, and yelling at the top of their lungs. Yes, our DI's had a highly elevated volume of dialogue, but the purpose behind their communication was empowerment. Everything our drill instructors did had a greater purpose. Their words, their body language, and their actions did more than just instruct us; they molded us. Marine leaders do not use communication merely to give orders to the troops.

They use it to empower their Marines during the most challenging situations. Marine Corps legend, Lewis B Puller, harnessed the power of dynamic communication. Affectionately known to his men as "Chesty," because of his huge barrel-shaped chest, he served our great nation for thirty-seven years. Starting out as an enlisted man, he worked his way up to the rank of a three-star general.

Lieutenant General Puller is synonymous with Marine Corps leadership. Among his numerous decorations, he was awarded five Navy Crosses, the Bronze Star, and the Purple Heart. He was a true Master of Communication, empowering his Marines during the toughest circumstances. This became evident during some of the bloodiest battles of World War II and the Korean War.

Imagine for a moment that you are a young Marine in Chesty's command. You are in sub-zero temperatures at the Chosin Reservoir in Korea. Thousands of miles from home, you stand on enemy soil with your fellow Marines, running out of food and ammunition. You are vastly outnumbered, and the odds are that you will not survive through the day. How do you feel? The most common answer I receive is, "Scared."

How important would your leader's communication be to you at this moment in your life? As legend has it, Chesty boldly assessed the dire situation for his Marines and addressed them with, "They are in front of us, behind us, and we are flanked on both sides by an enemy that outnumbers us 29 to 1." If you were one of the Marines in his ranks, this might not have been the dialogue you wanted to hear. But it was crystal clear. There were no misunderstandings or misinterpretations. Their situation was bleak.

With lives on the line, Chesty did not end his speech there. Moving beyond basic communication, he added seven words of dynamic communication as he finished addressing his Marines, and belted out, "They can't get away from us now!" How powerful was that extra dialogue to the men of 1st Marine Regiment? It was life-changing. The Marines not only won the battle, but they destroyed seven enemy divisions in the process. While the Marines lost 836 lives during this battle, the enemy suffered losses of nearly 35,000.

Chesty's Marines looked to him for inspiration and motivation. But he delivered more than that by empowering them with every well-placed word. With dynamic communication, he enhanced their belief levels about their circumstances and empowered them to achieve more than they thought possible.

Leadership Link What are your words of empowerment when your team needs you the most?

My devotion to this level of communication did not end when my tour of duty did. It has remained with me, and I have applied it to every aspect of my personal and professional life. Dynamic communication does not happen by chance, it happens by choice. Successful leaders do not empower people as a side effect of their words, their body language, and their actions. It is the driving purpose every time they communicate. Are you ready to improve the level of communication in your organization?

IMPROVING COMMUNICATION

Teaching leaders the importance of sending the right message, I typically encounter the universal acknowledgement, "I need to improve my communication skills." Leaders absolutely need to focus on improving their dialogue, because everything they say and do is constantly under scrutiny; analyzed and interpreted by everyone receiving their message.

Leadership Link Crystal-clear communication will remove misunderstandings, misinterpretations, and mistakes.

Required to speak in many settings, leaders communicate one-on-one, to teams, at meetings, and through various forms of correspondence. Improving basic communication skills is essential, and it starts by realizing communication is always a two-way process. It is never enough just to be heard; leaders must ensure that they have been understood.

Often times, many leaders look back on conversations and wish they had phrased things differently. The moment the words left their mouths, they knew they were not going to be interpreted as well as they had hoped. But hope is not a viable strategy when so much rides on developing dialogue that delivers a powerful message. To improve your communication skills, focus on three simple steps.

The 3 Steps to Improving Basic Communication:

1. Listen

2. Prepare

3. Deliver

Listen

Leaders must pay close attention to what people have to say. But they often mistake hearing for listening. Hearing is nothing more than registering the sounds entering your ears. Listening requires more; it requires focus. It requires a leader to be in the moment.

Listening allows a leader to connect with the audience and understand their story, through their verbal and non-verbal signals. Listening allows a leader to anticipate the receiver's viewpoint and feelings, formulate a deeper message, and increase the chances of empowering people.

Prepare

Leaders must plan their communication, especially when delivering a powerful message. Too many try to "wing-it" when they share important dialogue with their teams, and thus the results are often less than anticipated. Being prepared allows a leader to understand every audience, stay on target with key points, and achieve the desired outcomes.

While some instances might not allow a leader to fully develop a plan for communication, a leader who focuses on improving basic communication skills will always feel more prepared to interact with people, turning impromptu situations into empowering exchanges.

Deliver

Leaders must do more than speak. They need to make an impact. Everything has led to this moment; the moment of transferring a planned message to the audience. Rather than over-emphasizing problems, successful communicators deliver powerful solutions.

In addition to providing the necessary statistics to support the message, leaders who share relatable stories increase their connection to their audiences. Personal stories and passion resonate deeper than charts and graphs. Express meaning with conviction in your delivery and you will connect the importance of your message to the goals of the organization and the goals of your audience.

Leadership Link Improving communication is an everyday activity for leaders.

DYNAMIC COMMUNICATION

As a professional speaker, personal coach, and corporate trainer, my ability to deliver a powerful message, each time I communicate, is paramount. My team depends on my capability to provide dynamic communication, giving empowering messages to people to achieve greater results. Of course, isn't that what every leader should be striving for when they communicate?

I think it is fair to say all organizations would benefit from leaders who placed an emphasis on high levels of communication. But understanding the need for empowering people and carrying it out are two different things. Even the leaders who see the value in dynamic communication are often ill-prepared to follow through with it.

The first step to developing dynamic communication is to view every interaction as an opportunity to make a significant impact in the life of the person with whom you are connecting. No matter how brief the dialogue, leaders must possess a desire to empower that person, team, or audience.

As I became more aware of the dynamic possibilities with my own communication, I looked for common denominators I could easily repeat to achieve high levels of empowerment. I analyzed how my words, body language, and actions affected people and influenced them to reach for new heights.

I narrowed my style of dynamic communication to three main points. Not only could I intertwine these elements into virtually any conversation, and see results, but I could develop other leaders to do the same for their teams. Now, if I could create a way for them to remember these three points.

In the Marine Corps, we were required to remember many important things. Everything from understanding how our rifles operated to the function of our back-packs, had an acronym to help with memorization.

Rifle: LMGAS - **L**ightweight, **M**agazine-fed, **G**as-operated, **A**ir-cooled, **S**houlder-fired weapon

Back Pack: ALICE - **A**ll-purpose, **L**ight-weight, **I**ndividual **C**arrying **E**quipment

As seen in Chapter 1, I shared the acronym for remembering the 14 Leadership Traits of the Marine Corps - JJ DID TIE BUCKLE. It goes without saying that I would use an easy-to-remember acronym to keep dynamic communication on the forefront of leaders' thoughts and remind them to add these elements into their conversations.

BEC - The Elements of Dynamic Communication:

- Believe

- Encourage

- Challenge

Most leaders communicate about what they find to be wrong, and people usually stop wanting to hear more from these leaders. To empower, when you search for what has been done right and build on it, people will start to look forward to hearing more from you. Believe in people, encourage them to grow, and challenge them to unleash their true potential.

Believe

Leaders need to let people know they believe in them, and they matter. A leader's accomplishments and expertise have less of an impact than the expression of a sincere belief in an individual.

Expressing belief in someone is a powerful tool for a leader. It communicates trust, which is one of the strongest connections a leader can make with their team members. Belief validates people and helps them to draw on their own strengths to successfully navigate through difficult circumstances.

A leader's belief in someone must be genuine and authentic; it cannot be faked. When leaders show a belief in others, it also communicates a belief in themselves. It shows people you possess a confidence and certainty about your own abilities.

To be successful, leaders must believe in the individuals on their teams, the team as a whole, their organization, and themselves.

Encourage

Leaders who encourage people, help bring about significant enhancements in the lives of others. Encouragement provides people with the ability to make shifts. Encouragement gives people the power to dynamically alter their behaviors, their results, and their destiny.

Most people feel overwhelmed and overworked. The challenges of life causes many to experience discouragement, which creates lackluster performance and poor attitudes. Leaders who encourage people to make the necessary enhancements to succeed, make them feel stronger, more energized, and more excited. When people are encouraged, they find the inner fortitude to make things happen; things that would have seemed impossible unless they were encouraged with dynamic communication.

Leaders who want to encourage people must invest the time to get to know them. Communicate with the purpose of gaining a deeper understanding of their challenges. Get to know co-workers as people, not just employees. You might be surprised at what you discover, as they begin to communicate suggestions for greater possibilities.

Leadership Link

The cost to show appreciation... $0.

The return... priceless!

Challenge

Leaders who challenge people, do much more than "dare" them to grow. They empower them to develop. Presenting the right challenge to someone can reiterate a strong belief in them, encourage them to make positive enhancements, and enable them to see their true potential. Empowering someone might actually allow him or her to exceed their potential.

To challenge someone, you must engage your people in deeper levels of communication and search for the areas that mean the most to them. Actively seek areas where people have stalled, and where they have reached a plateau in their own growth. These are the areas where you can help them to overcome the obstacles in their own path to greatness.

Great leaders empower others with the solutions needed to overcome their obstacles, to grow, and to develop. Communication is one of the few components of leadership always in your control. You can provide dynamic communication that empowers everyone you encounter.

As leaders we must transform our communication and become more dynamic, empowering our team members every time we speak. Like a caterpillar metamorphosing into a butterfly, work on your communication and transform into the leader your team needs. There are significant benefits to dynamic communication.

The Benefits of Dynamic Communication:

- Inspires the team
- Causes the team to think... Think GREAT
- Encourages the team to take action
- Connects the team emotionally

Dynamic communication will begin a ripple effect throughout your organization, empowering people and encouraging them to follow your lead – to dynamically communicate, too. Imagine working in an environment of consistent dynamic communication from the entire team.

Steps to Dynamic Communication:

- Find reasons to praise your team
- Share your identity: Mission, Vision, Core Values
- Talk more about goals

Empowering your people through communication is a necessary step on your leadership expedition. But now, let's take the next step to empowerment and learn how to cultivate our people.

LEADERSHIP STEPS

COMMUNICATION

Elite Leadership Step – Assess Your Communication

- Identify the type of communication most prevalent in your organization.

  ☐ POOR   ☐ BASIC   ☐ DYNAMIC

  Next, using a scale of 1-10 (10 being best), rank the caliber of each:

Timely	_____	Collaborative	_____
Relevant	_____	Tactful	_____
Concise	_____	Positive	_____
Clear	_____	Follow-Up	_____
Complete	_____	Feedback	_____

Additional Steps

- **Issues:** Identify the top three communication issues facing your organization and how to enhance or remove each one.

- **B.E.C.:** Get off-site with your people, one-on-one, for some dynamic communication. Genuinely, let them know how much you believe in them, while you encourage them to make significant enhancements, and challenge them to grow and develop.

- **1 + 2:** Use issues to empower. Encourage your people to bring two solutions for every issue they discover. Not one, but two!

Chapter 8

Cultivation

Train People to Know More. Develop People to Grow More.

Teamwork! Let's say it again. Teamwork. This one word conjures up positive feelings of camaraderie and success, energy and excitement. Imagine what your organization would be like, if it were filled with driven, self-starting team players who all strive for excellence. The possibilities would be limitless. But that is not necessarily what occurs in most organizations.

Coaching, mentoring, and guiding powerful, dynamic teams is the aspiration of anyone who embraces the role of a leader. But instead, most leadership duties revolve around monitoring groups of people who struggle to work together and who barely fulfill the minimum requirements of their job descriptions.

Teamwork is an integral part of an organization's success. Transforming a group into a cohesive team requires much more than training. It requires a commitment greater than improving job skills; it requires the development (cultivation) of each person, personally and professionally. Cultivation allows team members and leaders to band together, maximizing their efficiencies and achieving common objectives. The benefits of teamwork are too important to take a casual approach.

THE IMPORTANCE OF CULTIVATION

If you are about to fly in an aircraft, how would you feel knowing that eighteen-year old's are controlling air traffic? Would anyone in their right mind give a headset to a teenager and put them up in the tower to control air traffic? At first thought, it makes no sense, but it happens every day in the military. I was eighteen when I reported for duty in the control tower of the Marine Corps Air Station in Yuma, Arizona.

I only received about four months of ATC training. While intensive, I do not believe it was my training that empowered me to be in the tower. I was certainly not ordered to be up there. I was inspired to be up there because I was developed to think and act as a leader. I was trained at my job (ATC) but developed to be a leader (people). It was my development that allowed me to do more with my training.

This is a concept I refer to as the *Engagement Ring*. Just as the Chinese philosophy of Yin and Yang describes how seemingly opposite forces may actually be complementary and are required for balance, I have found the same to be true of training and development. Most leaders only provide half of the equation, offering training, but failing to develop their people to think and act as leaders. Even if you have the best training program in the world but neglect to develop your people, you still have only completed 50% of the equation. In grade school that's an "F."

Leaders often wonder why their teams are not as productive as they could be and not as engaged as they should be. Most people are trained, so a lack of training is not the culprit. It is the lack of cultivation, the leadership development of the team, that is the primary cause of such little productivity and engagement in the workplace. Before I was trained with my rifle, I was introduced to leadership traits. Before I was trained to use my gas mask, I was taught leadership principles. Before I was trained to do my job (air traffic control), I was developed to perform as a leader, even though I had no one reporting to me.

Leadership Link Developing your people is not always easy, but it is always worth it.

One of the best ways to become a better leader is to continually develop your people to think and act as leaders. You must teach them about leadership, allowing them to become fluent in speaking leadership.

LATIN LESSON

DOCENDO DISCIMUS

Learning by Teaching

You can develop leaders by talking more about it: your definition of what it means to be a leader in your organization, your traits and your principles. Conduct leadership meetings to pull together your people, so they speak exclusively about leadership. The best way to grow as a leader is to teach about it.

FARMING FOR SUCCESS

Studies show that nearly 40 percent of employees are dissatisfied with their bosses, and over 70 percent are unhappy at their current jobs. I have yet to meet a leader who set out to create feelings of dissatisfaction and unhappiness. But these are the unfortunate side effects when leaders do not understand the importance of developing their people. Develop your team by cultivating them.

Because most people do not associate cultivation with people, let's take a look at this word to discover why it is so critical for planting leadership seeds throughout your organization.

cultivate

verb

- To promote or **foster** growth.
- To **prepare** and work on.
- To **grow** and **care** for.
- To **raise** under conditions you can control.
- To **develop** or **improve**.

According to this definition, cultivating sounds like farming. Truth be told, the role of a leader is much like that of a farmer; someone who fosters, prepares, grows, cares for, raises, develops, and improves. The similarities are uncanny. Are you cultivating your people? Let's take a look at the characteristics of a successful farmer and a successful leader.

A Successful Farmer:

- Pays close attention to the crops

- Is aware of surrounding elements

- Assesses their environment

- Strives for a healthy yield

- Prepares for a great future

A Successful Leader:

- Pays close attention to the team – COMMUNICATION

- Is aware of surrounding elements – IN's, ON's, OUT'S

- Assesses their environment – CULTURE

- Strives for a healthy yield – TRAINING

- Prepares for a great future – DEVELOPING

How important is cultivation to a farmer? About 150 plant species make up the world's food supply. More specifically, three "mega-crops," made up of rice, wheat, and maize, account for over half of the world-wide food production. It would be fair to say the cultivation of these crops is a top priority. When a farmer fails to implement proper growing techniques, it can impact many lives.

Over seven billion people populate the earth and the survival of the entire human race depends on our ability to produce enough food to sustain all of these lives. Unattended crops will fail to grow, just as an unattended team will fail to develop. Furthermore, the neglect of the land will result in soil erosion, negatively impacting growth for future years. The same happens in businesses every day when cultivation is ignored.

Leadership Link Leaders are superheroes with the power to cultivate others.

DON'T TRAIN LEADERS – DEVELOP THEM

Lately, the terms training and development have slowly become synonymous, and nothing could be farther from the truth. Working with countless organizations, I have observed virtually every type of leadership training program in existence. Unfortunately, most of them do not come close to helping to grow their leaders. Surveys, charts, and graphs do little to develop the skills of a leader. Worse yet, most training programs are rarely perceived as being beneficial.

Do not get me wrong, training serves a purpose and can be an effective tool, especially for improving the job proficiencies of your team members. But developing leaders and promoting empowerment will not happen merely in a classroom setting. Training reaffirms how to, while development instills why to. According to Forbes, organizations spend around "$130 billion worldwide" on corporate training and "the #1 areas of spending is management and leadership (35%)."

Unfortunately, the only consistent benefactor is usually the training industry, not the organization paying for the sessions, or the leaders who attend them. Development is an ongoing journey. The destination is progress, improvement, and growth. Training ends, whereas development continues. The biggest problem with training leaders is that most of the "leadership trainers" have had little to no formal leadership development themselves.

The differences between training and development:

Train	Develop
Process	People
Present	Future
Teach	Transform
Seeing inside the box	Envisioning outside the box
Tests knowledge	Tests understanding
Excepted standards	Unexpected potential
Status quo	Status grow
Indoctrinate	Innovate
Leadership position	Leadership purpose
Addresses problems	Identifies solutions
Employs people	Empowers People

Training is often a one-dimensional, one-directional undertaking that involves someone standing in front of a podium, using a strict agenda of topics to instruct the audience. The vast majority of training sessions fail because they take place within a lackluster environment, and they tend to focus on past failures as signs of what to avoid. Even the leaders who passionately want to grow and develop their skills usually dread traditional, lackluster trainings.

Because they do not perceive the value, the only things they focus on avoiding are training sessions. These same leaders will enthusiastically participate in the development of their skills, in an environment conducive to growth. Train your people to know more about their jobs; develop them to know more about their people. Leadership is the "people" business.

Cultivation is a shared process of discovery for everyone. Multi-dimensional in nature, it provides coaching, mentoring, and guiding. Focusing on real-life examples, leadership development concentrates all efforts on future needs and current progress. Development does not deal in the avoidance of issues, but rather a proactive approach to uncover new solutions.

The objective of training is to standardize, and to adapt to the status quo through procedures and best practices. While that is important, the priority of cultivation is different, embracing a "status grow" approach by identifying the unique attributes of each person. A leader might guide the session, but development occurs when everyone is encouraged to participate and share their own successes and failures, with the outcome being focused on growth.

Leadership language is paramount. True cultivation sessions occur in uniquely designed environments, where everyone is taught how to speak "Leading." Job training serves an immediate need, but having your people developed as leaders serves a life-long purpose for those who receive it.

Cultivation is not something to take lightly; for a farmer or a leader. Farmers have techniques to provide proper cultivation: adding nutrients to the soil, composting, planting cover crops, and mulching. In addition to being aware of the techniques available to cultivating a team, leaders must also watch out for the pitfalls, like falling into the *training trap*.

THE TRAINING TRAP

When I speak to leaders about the strategies they employ for building their teams, most proudly refer to some form of staff training they have scheduled, conducted, or recommended. While training has its merits, mistaking it for cultivating can lead to a dysfunctional team, lackluster results, and unwanted frustrations.

The problem with training is it is usually focused on job skills (not people skills) and often is an attempt to prevent everything from going wrong. Issues on the production line result in training classes on efficiencies, while problems in the sales department usher in new sales trainings to fix weak prospecting, minimal contacting, and a lack of follow-up.

In most organizations, training is not held in the highest regard, often perceived synonymously with errors, mistakes, and reprimands. Sometimes implemented poorly, and rarely providing the long-term, permanent solutions it was intended for, most training falls short of its objectives. Worse yet, when it fails to fully resolve an issue, people begin to have the perception that it has little value. Because most training is designed to fix broken things, it does not make sense that this is your only team-building tactic.

Organizations spend hundreds of millions of dollars every year on training programs, yet they still experience the same mediocre results from their teams. Training has not solved the disengagement epidemic in the workplace. When properly implemented, in conjunction with development programs, training is a viable way to increase knowledge. The other half of the equation, cultivating, increases growth through teamwork, as it promotes deeper levels of understanding about leadership and people.

Training – Knowing More

Cultivating – Growing More

Training is necessary in any organization. When done right, it creates higher levels of efficiency, increased confidence levels in team members, and greater customer satisfaction. When implementing any form of training in your organization, keep some basic techniques at the forefront of your program to ensure that it empowers people:

- Always have a definitive outcome

- Understand the specific needs of the student

- Provide regular follow up

Whether I was a young Marine, an employee at K-Mart, the vice president of a multi-million-dollar company, or the owner of my own business, training has been and always will be a powerful tool for enhancing my performance and the performance of those around me. But the development of myself and my team is what allows us to do more with our training.

In many organizations, leadership development focuses only on a few select individuals. With the desire to enhance their leaders' skills, internal training often centers too much around improving procedural responsibilities. Instructing someone how to manage schedules, comply with regulations, and hire and fire, in accordance with company policies, does not make for a better leader.

Leadership Link There are no natural-born leaders. We all have the ability to learn how to be better leaders.

STARTING TO CULTIVATE

Cultivation always starts at the top. Just as a farmer rises at the crack of dawn to tend to his fields, a leader must always be prepared to rise to the exciting challenges of cultivating the team. You do not need to put on a pair of overalls, hop on a tractor, and plow the fields to begin this process, although it just might leave a lasting impression on your team.

Cultivation, in a manner that fundamentally causes people to become better leaders and improves their teamwork, will not be found in a training session. It will not be discovered in a PowerPoint presentation or in the pages of a handbook. Creating a cohesive unit, in an environment of learning and empowerment, is a process that takes place by consistently applying the ABC's.

The ABC's of Cultivating:

    A. **A**chieve **A**uthenticity

    B. **B**e the **B**eacon

    C. **C**reate **C**amaraderie

Achieve Authenticity

Developing a team of people who are genuine, reliable, and dedicated is not as easy as it might seem. Leaders are not typically handed a dream team upon assuming a leadership position, but they are more than capable of developing one, provided they can achieve high levels of authenticity among all team members.

Creating an environment where people can be authentic, operating with trust and honesty, will develop team members who are able to perform naturally as part of a unit. Authenticity allows team members to provide honest feedback, leading to more viable solutions. Honesty leads to truth and truth brings forth integrity. Authenticity allows these characteristics to form an unbreakable foundation among your people. Imagine having a team of genuine, trustworthy, honest, reliable, and dedicated team members, all focused on common goals.

Achieving authenticity allows leaders to develop stronger teams, but it requires deeper levels of dialogue. It cannot be achieved solely through notes, letters, and e-mails. To raise teamwork to this level, leaders must engage in meaningful discussions with their people as a whole and with each team member individually.

Great leaders are great listeners. They use questions to gain a better understanding of their people, their organizations, and the unique challenges within their environments. Leaders should be cautious about using questions that can be interpreted as forms of manipulation, interrogation, or finding fault.

Great teams are built upon open discussions, free from agendas and pressure. Striving for genuineness, leaders should use questions to build trust, loyalty, and respect. I ask questions, not because the answer is of the greatest importance, but because achieving authenticity is my highest priority. I ask questions like, "Can you share with me more about that?" "Do you have a solution?" and "What can we do better?"

Teams that operate with distrust and dissatisfaction tend to increase frustrations and negative behaviors throughout their organizations. Tracing the roots of their behaviors often points to the quality of the dialogue occurring within their teams. When leaders fail to develop deeper forms of dialogue, they will fail to achieve authenticity within their ranks.

Leaders who desire to understand situations better and allow their staff to share their own unique experiences, will open up lines of communication to help bond team members together with the perspective of discovering solutions.

Leadership Link Provide the support necessary to minimize conflicts and maximize results, together as a team.

Be the Beacon

To a ship at sea, navigating through a dark and foreboding storm, there is no greater sight than the beacon of a lighthouse. More than being a guide, it instantaneously fills the crew with hope and relief. As a leader, be the beacon for your team; the shining light of guidance and support.

Teams are usually assigned priority objectives, shouldering much of the workload and stress. They need leaders who project the illumination of positivity; not the spotlight of interrogation. Leaders are the guiding light, helping their people to stay focused on the mission and purpose behind their actions.

How do leaders stay focused on the vision of their organization, while trying to handle the myriad of details and requirements of leading a team? Invest time to share the big picture of your organization with your team members. Share the goals, the aspirations, and the greater purpose of why everyone has been united into a cohesive team. Share your plan and make sure to discuss their *Who*.

To cultivate a team, leaders are required to inspire, motivate, and influence people. When their crew experiences a lack of clarity and a decrease in self-confidence, it is up to the leader to transform them into people with higher belief levels and increased commitment.

Keeping them focused on the big picture ensures that the small things do not become overwhelming roadblocks. Constantly sharing the greater purpose with your team will keep them moving forward, toward the important goals of the organization. But sharing the big picture is not only important for the team members; it is also a priority for the leaders.

It is easy to feel off-balance when you juggle many items and spin many plates. I have always found that focusing on the big picture provided me with the stability I needed to be a better leader for my team, and to constantly shine a light of guidance.

Leadership Link Call daily meetings to review the big picture. Seize the opportunity to reset priorities as team members become reenergized with purpose, clarity, and conviction.

Create Camaraderie

Serving in the military allowed me to experience the highest levels of camaraderie. Training and preparing for combat develops a bond virtually impossible to duplicate in the civilian sector. I share a kindred spirit with my Marine brothers and sisters, and with my fellow veterans. This unbreakable bond is one of the things I miss the most from my service days. It is also one of the things I constantly seek out.

While your staff will not likely be facing enemy forces, creating camaraderie will take teamwork to an entirely new level for your organization. This bond does not occur because people get along. It does not happen by spending most of your day with someone, nor is it merely the spirit of good fellowship.

True camaraderie is the mutual trust and deep friendship that evolves between people who believe wholeheartedly in their purpose, and overcome the challenges they face together, while fully engaged in their mission. To achieve this level of teamwork requires leaders to do more than just promote corporate activities such as sports teams and community service events, which are valuable, and we did both in the Marine Corps.

The bond that develops deep levels of loyalty, dedication, and commitment can only be achieved by challenging the team. But most leaders try to avoid this technique, fearing backlash from their staff. Here is a little leadership secret: great teams want to be challenged; they do not want you to dump your challenges on them. Great teams have a tremendous amount of respect for the leader who believes in them enough to create the opportunities for them to grow.

We need team members who want to be inspired, motivated, and influenced. We want them to look forward to showing up every day and creating new ideas. Leaders must not set impossible challenges, but rather pay keen attention to setting achievable benchmarks that will cause each member on their team to develop, personally and professionally.

Leaders possess the ability to influence people. But many waste that gift and keep their teams trapped in mediocrity. Challenge them to do things they do not immediately believe they can do. Leaders do more than provide motivation:

they provide opportunities to step up to the next level. Challenging your team is not just a reflection of your belief in them, it is also your belief in yourself.

Begin by assigning smaller, difficult projects to your team and allow them to display their creativity and initiative. Set timelines to create a sense of urgency and to keep them on track. This will help prepare them to be a part of your Think Tank sessions, coming up in Chapter 9.

Overcoming challenges together creates a strong bond and transforms your people from spectators to team players. Give them a chance to grow and they will provide you with opportunities to do it more often. Yes, there is always a risk involved when you issue tough projects. You are probably qualified to do it faster, do it better, and do it with less stress. But your role as a leader is to cultivate a team, not to enable a comfort zone.

Leadership Link Cultivating our people increases the likelihood of forming productive teams.

You cannot successfully take everything on yourself and hope to build deep bonds among your team. You cultivate a team by creating camaraderie.

CULTIVATION BUILD TEAMS

When we encourage our people to work together, share ideas, discover new solutions, and rely on each other, the incredible side effect of this process is teamwork. There is no magic to team-building. It is something that occurs when leaders truly care about their people on deeper levels.

When you begin building cohesive teams, remember these tips to enhance cultivation as you get to know your people:

- Discover similar values
- Remember the smallest details about them (and their Who's)
- Practice patience
- Ask deeper questions

- Let your guard down

- Ask why they are still there (what keeps them at your organization?)

Cultivating people provides distinct advantages, not only to the members of the team, but also to anyone who encounters them. How important is "cultivation" to a leader? Simply put, it means the difference between growing an organization, or watching it wither and die.

The Benefits of Teamwork:

- Synergy

- Effectiveness

- Resourcefulness

Synergy

The same fingers that can point the blame at others, can join together with the hands of other positive team members to create an unbreakable bond. A synergistic team achieves peak performance by understanding their roles, sharing the workload, and collaborating together for the greater good of the organization.

Effectiveness

Most people go to work. Effective teams excitedly show up to make an impact. They perform at the highest levels of excellence, striving to increase each other's achievements, which eliminates wasted time and increases results.

Resourcefulness

Members of dynamic teams present solutions, discovering new ways of doing things. Resourceful teams strive to see the process of each project through to completion.

How would it feel to lead a synergistic, effective, and resourceful team? It feels GREAT! But leaders who fail to create an environment of teamwork, have usually failed to put in the work required to properly develop a team at this level. Teamwork does not magically occur by appointing people to a roster. It is the result of cultivating the talent and untapped potential of each member.

Leadership
Link Leaders cultivate their people to form a team that works together, looking out for each other, no matter what circumstances they face.

Cultivating a team is typically a new discipline for many leaders. It will take time to become natural at cultivating the individuals on your team, but the results will be well worth your efforts. Cultivating allows your team to grow. Most importantly, cultivation leads to collaboration.

LEADERSHIP STEPS

CULTIVATION

Elite Leadership Step – Building a Cohesive Unit

- Identify what you and your leaders are currently doing to transform your group of employees into a cohesive team. What do you need to implement to ensure that this transformation happens?

  Perhaps shared goals, cross-training, off-site activities, and "team" meetings should be incorporated more. Begin to "Share the Podium" with your people, allowing them to develop by permitting their voices to be heard.

Additional Steps

- **Training 1.0:** Describe your current training programs and how they can be enhanced to not only allow people to know more, but to become more empowering. Is there a schedule of training for the next twelve months? Is it known by the entire team?

- **Training 2.0:** Get off-site with your people to discuss the training and cross-training programs required to achieve greater results and encourage high levels of teamwork.

- **Developing:** Describe your current development programs – how you help your team to grow as people – personal and professional development. How can you enhance these programs? Do you need to create some development programs?

Chapter 9

Collaboration

Unleash the Power of People.

From the outside, my daughter's preschool was peaceful and tranquil, beautiful and inviting. But as I entered the building to drop her off, I encountered an eruption of chaos; a mixture of talking, crying, laughing, and the sound of toys crashing to the floor. In her classroom, the communication elevated as I was surrounded by four-year old's, all interrupting each other and determined to be the first to share their vitally important stories with me.

Taking my daughter to school provided me with a unique insight into the challenges of getting people to work together. Working together is one thing; collaborating is an entirely different thing. The whirlwind of uncontrolled dialogue and energy I witnessed each day made me question if I could last more than fifteen minutes in a room filled with these toddlers. The answer was important because I was scheduled to volunteer as a "teacher's assistant" one upcoming morning.

The day rolled around, and I somewhat reluctantly reported for duty. I admit I had some reservations, perhaps some anxiety about stepping into an environment with no structure, but rather a free-for-all of attitudes and emotions. Does that sound like any work environments you have experienced?

As expected, chaos ensued. But to my surprise, it only lasted for about the first 15-20 minutes. Once the impact of being dropped off had subsided, I watched a group of people begin the process of collaboration. Influencing others, they placed a great emphasis on encouraging the group to see things from a new point of view as they worked on their projects: building forts, making crafts, and orchestrating other activities. They also provided support to help in the achievement of better results.

You may think I'm referring to the teachers, but it happened with the children. The teachers did a great job too, but it was natural for most of the four-year old's to try work as a team. They were passionate, focused (for small amounts of time), and creative. Too many leaders experience a lack of this collaborative spirit in the workplace.

With the guidance of their teachers, the children accomplished amazing works of art, towering formations of blocks, and physics-defying structures. They might not have gotten along every step of the way, and there was some crying and hurt feelings, but they produced incredible results. The preschoolers worked together toward a greater purpose, even if they were the only ones who understood that purpose.

After three hours, I came out with a different perspective on the unlimited possibilities of collaboration. I also developed a much deeper appreciation for the teachers and the patience they displayed with their tiny teams. They used their position of leadership to do more than force the children to cooperate and coordinate their efforts. They encouraged them to collaborate, innovate, and achieve something new, better, and greater.

The teachers taught them how to work together as a team and create something that their individual efforts could not have produced. If collaboration can be achieved in a preschool, imagine the possibilities when it is implemented in your organization. The benefits of fostering innovative results will have a long-term impact on the team, the leaders, and the company. Collaboration empowers people.

Leadership Link Collaboration is more than working together. It unleashes the power of people.

THE IMPORTANCE OF COLLABORATION

The first step in the collaboration process is to ensure that every leader and every team member understands the importance of working together – team work. Collaboration is best achieved by a team, not a group.

LATIN LESSON

OPUS UNA

Work Together

Collaboration is a unification tool, bringing your team closer together – making their connection even greater. Rising levels of trust among the team will lead to you and your people working together in a different capacity, positioning the organization to achieve unparalleled results.

Achieving and maintaining an environment that promotes and supports high-level results through creativity and innovation is difficult to consistently accomplish when a deeper understanding of authentic collaboration is not attained. The benefits of collaboration are too great to ignore.

The Benefits of Collaboration:

- Supports organizational goals
- Enhances team member strengths
- Promotes forward-thinking
- Increases an organization's relevancy
- Identifies best practices
- Improves retention

Every leader would readily accept the benefits of collaboration, but to guarantee that it occurs, we need to first take a closer look at the definition of this word to understand how to evoke it.

collaboration

verb

- To work together for a common purpose.
- The action of coming together to produce something.
- To work jointly in an intellectual endeavor.
- To bring people together for innovative ideas.

Again, when it comes to empowering people, we see another verb. We cannot afford to sit back and hope it miraculously happens. We must take action. Working with leaders to create the environments that support collaboration, I quickly identify two types of leaders.

- Issue-Focused
- Solution-Focused

Some leaders focus exclusively on their issues, unable to break out of everything weighing them down. Their focus can be perceived as negative, whining, and complaining. It can push people away. For collaboration to work, we need to pull people together to harness their innovative ideas to discover solutions for every issue – and opportunity.

Collaboration will not only pave the way to remove the OUT's plaguing your organization, but it will position your team to find ways to turn new opportunities into realities. As the VP of the media company, I was there when the world was switching from standard definition to high definition.

Failing to collaborate and discover how to stay ahead of the rapidly evolving technology curve caused many of our competitors to go out of business. Because our team of leaders regularly focused on innovative ideas to maximize this new opportunity, we discovered ways to offer new services to our clients – we became even more relevant.

By finding creative solutions, we ushered in high-definition editorial, motion graphics, closed-captioning, and digital film archiving and restoration. We grew when many other businesses withered away. Discovering solutions through the art of collaboration is not an option for leaders. It is an obligation that cannot be ignored because it is 100% an "ON" action. How, do I know it is, you ask?

It's right in the name of the action: COLLABORAT**ION**

It is also in the name of the result: SOLUT**ION**

Leadership Link Unify your team to divide their challenges, while multiplying their results.

UNDERSTANDING COLLABORATION

A lack of collaboration is costly to an organization and draining to its team members. Most leaders spend the majority of their time dealing with internal conflicts and problems. Meetings become a frustrating exercise in mistake-management, accounting for endless hours of repetitive discussions, with little-to-no resolution.

Most leaders whom I work with dedicate up to 50 percent (some spend more) of their time to handling the resolution of conflicts and customer satisfaction issues. If a leader earns $100,000 per year, the organization is paying upwards of $50,000 annually toward these activities and losing much more in missed opportunities.

Unfortunately, the high cost of a non-collaborative environment does not stop there. Organizations typically experience greater employee turnover and the loss of top talent. The expense of replacing a team member is often two to three times the cost of their annual salary. Without enthusiasm in the workplace, employees often have higher levels of absenteeism and lower levels of production.

Creating a collaborative environment will produce an immediate ROI as leaders dedicate their time to productive solutions that will eliminate the need for time-wasting activities, and support an exciting environment of creativity, growth, and success. This collaborative ROI comes from new opportunities, cost reductions, team optimization, and solid business decisions.

By now, every leader reading this book should be jumping at the opportunity to implement this strategy within their organization, right? Unfortunately, many fail to sustain this type of environment because they mistakenly confuse collaboration with coordination and cooperation. While both are needed to achieve true collaboration, they are merely the stepping stones to collaboration, and have distinct differences.

Coordination

This is the process of exchanging information and resources between individuals, teams, and organizations to accomplish a mutual objective. This process requires attention to detail and follow-through but does not strive to create something new through innovation.

Example: when a customer places an order, a team member coordinates its fulfillment with the supplier.

Cooperation

This is the ability for individuals to work together as a team for the completion of a common objective. This process requires teamwork and positive attitudes but does not strive to develop new systems to enhance results.

Example: when an order encounters an issue, team members cooperate to ensure that the issue is resolved, and the objective is achieved.

Collaboration

This is the collective creative energies generated by linking together the members of a team who are dedicated to uncovering new, innovative ideas and solutions for success and growth. This process requires a leader, a team, and a culture designed to support creativity and innovation.

Example: when ideas are needed to elevate customer satisfaction, and add depth to an organization's products, resources, and services, team members collaborate to discover viable ways to get there.

In addition to making the distinction between coordination and cooperation, leaders must also identify the enemy of collaboration and avoid it at all costs. I have found many leaders sacrifice collaboration for *consensus*; striving to make everyone "feel" good. Collaboration does not require everyone to agree; it does require everyone to set their sights on the greater solution, in an environment of trust and respect.

A collaborative team does not strive only to make friendships; it strives to make advancements. Proper collaboration, however, will produce camaraderie between the members of the team. But when consensus overrides collaboration, possibilities are reduced to compromises. Consensus often slows down momentum and allows for sub-par ideas to make it through the collaborative filters. Never lower the bar with collaboration.

Authentic collaboration is not easy to achieve, but it is absolutely worth the effort that will be put forth. Creating something that is larger than the individual efforts of each member provides a heightened sense of satisfaction and connects each person on the team at a deeper level. Being part of an innovative team is an exhilarating, life-changing feeling. It is highly empowering.

Leadership Link You cannot force collaboration; you can only inspire it.

THE LINK TO COLLABORATION

Creating and maintaining a collaborative environment might seem like a daunting task. But it is the result of transferring energy and power, from the leader to the team, in a way that creates increased momentum. To achieve the win-win results of "pulling" a team together for a higher purpose, let's take a quick look at the elements required to pull a freight train.

An average locomotive engine might pull 100 train cars, each weighing 50 tons. That is 5,000 tons or 10 million pounds. The idea of getting a train with smooth wheels, on a smooth track, to gain enough momentum to move could seem impossible. But it happens every day. Not only do these trains gain enough force to move forward, but they can travel at speeds of over 60 mph. The ability to pull this amount of weight involves the collective effort of each train car.

Without getting too deep into physics and the difference between static and kinetic friction, let's explore the connection between the engine and the boxcars, which allows the insurmountable weight of a freight train to start moving, pick up speed, and become virtually an unstoppable force. How would you like your team to be unstoppable?

One of the most important components of a train is the coupling; the "link" between the cars. How important is this link? The connection between each car must allow for movement – a range of motion. *Slack action* is the term used to describe the amount of free movement of one freight car before it transmits its motion to an adjoined car. If the connection is too rigid, it will prohibit any movement. Navigating around a curve would be impossible with no free movement.

Motion results from keeping the cars loosely coupled, which allows trains to bend around dangerous curves, and is also a vital component of starting the initial momentum. As the engine starts to move, the power of the locomotive transfers to each car, creating a wave of compressing couplings between all the cars. One at a time, they begin to move, causing motion in the other cars. The calculated space between the couplings allows for this movement and the transfer of power.

If every car was connected with a rigid, unmoving link, even a train with a powerful engine would fail to pull the weight behind it. The link of connected cars would merely become one large solid object, remaining motionless on the tracks, despite the engine exerting massive energy. I have met too many leaders who feel like this locomotive.

Like a fast-moving train, collaboration will take a lot of energy to get it started, but it is often impossible to stop the positive, forward-moving momentum, once it achieves high velocity. A leader is more like the conductor of a locomotive engine, striving to achieve the output of energy required to maintain consistent movement in the right direction. A leader is the first link in creating the collaborative environment in their organization.

I first experienced collaboration as a newly promoted Lance Corporal. One might think the Marine Corps has too rigid an environment for collaboration, but nothing could be farther from the truth. In 1988, I was deployed to the desert of Twentynine Palms, CA, to participate in Operation Gallant Eagle. In the sweltering heat, I joined thousands of other Marines for a two-week joint operation with the Army.

This exercise provided soldiers and Marines the opportunity to perform in a collaborative environment involving tactics and warfare. It was a massive operation, with battalions of infantry and air wing commands. Our leaders provided the opportunity for the troops to practice their existing procedures, while developing new strategies and techniques. This collaborative effort allowed the Army and the Marine Corps to "battle" each other, with the outcome of achieving higher effectiveness and efficiencies for both sides.

Who won the battle? Well, the answer is probably based on who you ask. According to the soldiers, the Army won. According to the Marines, the Marine Corps won. With collaboration, both sides ultimately won important victories for their organizations.

Leadership Link The outcome of collaboration is not just collaborating. The outcome is achieving greater results.

THE THINK TANK

So, you're sold on the idea of collaboration and the benefits it will bring to you, your team, and your organization. Understanding the power of making the leadership link to this fast-moving train is the first step. But how do you get it to leave the station?

A leader must establish the framework for collaboration in their environment. Merely pulling some people together as a committee to discuss things will not get the job done. Sustained, collaborative results require the formation of a Think Tank; a forward-thinking team that brings innovative ideas with authenticity, trust, experience, and passion.

When forming this high-caliber, solution-oriented team, you must raise the bar on attendance. Many leaders make the mistake of involving people only because they like them – their favorites. An effective Think Tank is not a group formed to make people feel good.

This unique gathering is not about the quantity of people in attendance. It is about the quality of the people in attendance. To achieve the results possible from a team of great thinkers, you must adhere to a high standard for inclusion in your Think Tank.

Criteria for a Successful Think Tank:

- Membership must be earned
- Objectives must be crystal-clear
- Time frames must be established
- Schedules must be set

Membership

Membership should be earned, never given. Form each Think Tank, comprised of your best people, not your best friends. Collaboration teams only work if every person brings their "A" game to the table. As their leader, it is your responsibility to form up the team required for innovative ideas.

Members need to exhibit the highest levels of respect for each other, understanding that their collective input is what will help each of them to arrive at the desired solution.

Objectives

Every Think Tank serves a purpose, and should have an outcome, which must be clearly communicated to each member of the team. Their role in the Think Tank should be directly linked to the objectives. By focusing on these priorities, a leader can eliminate the personal egos of the team members and increase the results from their professional input.

By clearly articulating the objective to be achieved in each session, you will ignite inspiration. Passion and dedication are contagious.

Time Frames

Setting time frames creates a sense of urgency. If the outcome is important enough to form a Think Tank, it is important enough to have timelines for the Think Tank session and the accomplishment of the objectives. Some time frames might be non-negotiable. If your Think Tank is unable to provide a solution by a specific date, you might lose a sale, or a customer.

Some timelines might be more forgiving. But to show that the outcome is important, establish time frames for all Think Tank objectives.

Schedules

Each Think Tank is typically comprised of leaders and top-talent team members who already have a full plate. Setting up a schedule for collaboration and for follow-up discussions will allow you to harness time mastery and keep your Think Tank team members from feeling overwhelmed.

Schedule the team to regularly review and evaluate the status of their innovative efforts. Schedules allow for balance by setting specific durations for each meeting, while establishing the much-needed accountability to stay on track.

Leadership Link Your ultimate success is based largely on the success of your daily schedule.

STARTING A THINK TANK

The impact of collaboration cannot be overstated. Studies show that this creative process can dramatically affect profitability, team member performance, growth, sales results, product development, customer satisfaction, and overall quality. Authentic collaboration is a key driver of success. But more importantly, it ushers in the highest levels of empowerment. So, particular attention should be paid to properly starting a solution-oriented team.

Providing the free-flowing innovation of ideas in a structured format requires a leader who is confident and creative. Leaders who are accustomed to a traditional "command and control" leadership style might find the collaborative process foreign to their way of operating, unless they can make the necessary shifts. Rigid leaders will have difficulty achieving consistent collaboration with their people.

To benefit from the collaborative efforts of your team, the starting steps are crucial. It is best to start with Level 1 Think Tanks. These sessions focus on smaller projects and assignments, such as issue resolutions and workflow enhancements. Before tackling highly technical objectives, I formed a Think Tank to discover permanent solutions to some of our internal workflow issues; ways to remove redundancies and eliminate mistakes.

Focusing on improving our internal efficiencies, with Level 1 Think Tanks, our collaborative team learned how to work together as we discovered out-of-the-box solutions to our own issues. As we shared innovative ideas, we focused on the creation of a checkpoint system to reduce errors made by our staff. By starting small, and then isolating our collaborative energies, we launched a system that reduced our errors by over 98 percent.

Regardless of the scope of the team's objectives, collaboration must always start at the top and have the full support of the entire leadership team. The actions and the words of the senior leaders will have a major impact on the innovative results the team achieves.

Collaborative teams must also be surrounded by trust and respect. Leaders should provide regular constructive feedback to the entire team to ensure they are on target with the assigned objectives. Trust will allow for crystal-clear communication in a safe environment; one that welcomes new ideas, no matter how bold or crazy.

Leaders should expect that certain contributions will cause some levels of disagreement and should be prepared to resolve conflict in a fair and productive manner. You will always get more out of authentic collaboration than you were expecting. In addition to fresh, new ideas, collaboration empowers everyone involved, directly and indirectly.

As the collaborative skills of your team grows, you will be able to launch Level 2 Think Tanks, focused on high-level growth ideas. Level 2 Think Tanks tackle both short-term and long-term goals, and everything from market expansion to new products and services.

Leadership Link While teamwork is a cornerstone of collaboration, innovative thinking helps to make each member of the team stronger.

THE POWER OF A THINK TANK

Collaboration exponentially increases the odds of maximizing organizational growth, as it positions leaders to work "ON" priority objectives. In today's fast-moving business environments, leaders need an edge. Those who are able to establish Think Tank teams, replacing uncertainty with clarity, and developing new ideas for success, gain that edge.

As an executive in the media industry, technology evolved quickly, and I watched businesses rise and fall. In 2009, most of our clients began the transition from standard definition (SD) to high definition (HD) formats for their broadcast projects; those airing on television and cable networks.

While the picture quality became a visually superior image, HD broadcasting presented many new variables which caused the transition to be more than a simple one-step process. Expensive new equipment and software presented additional learning curves. Many factors needed to be considered in order to achieve the desired results. Because this format was still relatively new, few were experts in this arena.

We needed to quickly elevate our relevancy to clients, if we expected them to remain our clients. The importance of our Think Tank grew as we addressed the upcoming technology trends. We identified our clients who would need

HD services, the equipment required, and what our obstacles would be. Most importantly, we aimed for viable solutions we could present to all of our clients.

For a few years, we had been servicing the "deliverable" media needs for South Park, the highest rated show for the Comedy Central Network. Deliverables are the final copies of the show and would be duplicated on various video formats. We successfully fulfilled every weekly order, but they were standard definition. The game was changing, and I knew the South Park team would be transitioning to high definition soon.

Not wanting to fall behind the technology curve, I took a proactive approach and called on my Think Tank team. During this Level 2 session, we discussed a strategy and designed specific options I could present to the South Park creative crew. I did not take for granted that their HD business would come to us. I wanted to position us to be their premiere choice.

After flushing out all of the variables, possible obstacles, and challenges with our Think Tank team, I confidently contacted their post-production supervisor and suggested we run a series of tests for their transition to high definition broadcasting. After the collective data was gathered, the South Park team made their decision.

On March 11, 2009, South Park aired episode 182 in HD. Not only did we continue to service all of their media deliverable needs, we also took their entire library of past episodes and up-converted everything to high definition. By enlisting the innovative and creative input of our Think Tank, the collaborative process allowed us to do more than just earn additional business, it positioned us to transform our entire organization, empowering our people in the process.

As your Think Tank collaborates and identifies the innovative ideas that will elevate your business, these new goals will go into your Flight Plan... every leader needs to *Have a Plan.*

LEADERSHIP STEPS

COLLABORATION

Elite Leadership Step – Form the Think TANK

• Prepare for unparalleled collaboration by selecting the members of your Think Tank teams. Identify team members and list why you specifically chose them. What traits and skills do they consistently bring to the table?

Get off-site with each one to share your desire to enlist them into a Think Tank and tell them why you chose them.

Additional Steps

• **Objectives:** With your team, identify the areas in your business that require collaboration. Perhaps topics such as future products and services, improving communication, raising team morale, and elevating customer service could use some innovative new insights.

• **Level 1:** Starting off on a smaller scale, use the "Criteria for a Successful Think Tank" to tackle the smaller projects for collaboration, such as workflow enhancements, improving scheduling, and upgrading systems.

• **Level 2:** Moving into a larger and more strategic scale, continue to use the "Criteria for a Successful Think Tank" to engage your team for the innovative ideas needed to achieve priority objectives such as your short-term and long-term goals, strategic planning, and market expansion.

Part IV

Exceed Possibilities

Part IV

Exceed Possibilities

The Breakthroughs for Magnifying Results.

Ask the members of any organization one simple question, "What should a leader do?" and you will discover a multitude of answers. Your team members, peers, supervisors, board members, and/or partners will all have a different set of ideas on the true expectations of a leader. Among many other things, leaders are expected to set goals, motivate, guide, resolve conflicts, develop strategy, enhance culture, and provide support.

But one response quickly sums up what a leader is ultimately responsible for: *results*. In many organizations, the desired results might not clearly be identified and the pressure of "hitting the target" can be overwhelming. "Black Monday," is the name given in the National Football League (NFL) on the day following the end of their regular season. This is the day when a number of head coaches are typically fired.

Were they good guys? Yes, I'm sure many were. Did they have an in-depth knowledge of football? Absolutely! Were they liked by their players? Probably. They were fired for one specific reason – they did not deliver results. It's highly unlikely that a coach who wins the Super Bowl will be let go after he delivers the big win – the desired results.

In today's highly competitive and unstable environments, I believe that successful leaders must strive to do more than just achieve results. Doing things better than the competition is rarely enough. Strong leaders position themselves to exceed possibilities, enabling their organizations to attain new opportunities and avoid potential threats.

Leaders are responsible for hitting the target. Those who lack the necessary accuracy, might soon find themselves looking for work elsewhere. The quality of leadership in an organization, more than any other component, determines success and failure. Leaders must be able to identify the target, achieve results, and exceed possibilities. Learning to hone your people skills will improve your chances for the breakthroughs you and your team need.

Leadership Link Leadership is a life-long journey of discovering ways to improve personally, while impacting everyone we encounter.

THE IMPORTANCE OF EXCEEDING EXPECTATIONS

If I ask you to name some great leaders, who comes to mind? They can be historical figures or modern-day. Regardless of where I am across the country, when I ask this question in my workshops and presentations, I typically hear the same names.

GREAT Leaders:

- Gandhi
- Martin Luther King Jr.
- Mother Teresa
- Abraham Lincoln
- Margaret Thatcher
- Winston Churchill
- Nelson Mandela

These leaders are considered great, not good. I have never asked anyone what they think of Martin Luther King Jr. and they replied with, "He's alright." No, they describe him as a great leader. While most of us are not trying to change the world, we do want to be better leaders at work. It pays to understand why so many consider so few to be so "great."

I believe that each of these leaders share some common characteristics that allowed them to exceed possibilities. These qualities are not only required on the global stage, but also in every environment when you want to take your team and your business to the next level.

GREAT Leaders:

- Go into the challenge - they do not run from it.

- Stay true to their vision - they share it regardless of their circumstances.

- Foster a lifestyle of leadership - they do not turn it off at 5 o'clock.

Most importantly, great leaders make an impact in the people they encounter. For leaders like Ghandi, MLK, and Mother Teresa, they exceeded expectations and their impact still lives on today. We need to strive, each day, to make an impact in their lives of those around us. Do we face different challenges than those leaders faced? Yes. Because our circumstances are probably not as severe, we owe it to ourselves and our teams to be impactful leaders.

If we are going to exceed possibilities, it makes sense to understand what a possibility is.

possibility

noun

- A thing that may happen or be the case.
- The state or condition of being possible.
- Something that might be done.
- The likelihood of something being true.

According to these definitions, every goal, objective, and project you are striving to complete "may happen" or "might be done." It also means that they may not happen or might not be done. Developing yourself and your team members will do much more than ensure that you accomplish your possibilities; it will position you to exceed them.

Leadership Link You cannot manage your way to greater results. You must lead your way there.

AIMING FOR SUCCESS

I slowly raised the barrel of my rifle, lining up my front sight post over the target in front of me. Mounted in large wooden frames, the paper targets featured various sizes and shapes, based on the distance from the impact zone. Two targets, the "B-Mod" and the "Dog" resembled the upper-torso of a person, while another, the "Able," featured various size circles.

The outer circle of the Able target had the widest radius but offered the least amount of points for striking inside of it. Each successive circle featured a smaller radius, but the number of points that could be earned increased. At the center of the target was the main objective – a solid black circle, twelve inches in diameter, worth the maximum of five points.

My results on the rifle range would do more than just qualify me as a rifleman. They would be an important step toward earning the title of U.S. Marine. As we stepped up to the first qualifying distance at 200 yards, the targets seemed to be hopelessly far off. After all, they were two football fields away. But that was only the first part of our qualification. We would soon move back to the 300-yard and then the 500-yard ranges.

I wanted to do more than just hit the target; I wanted as many bullseyes as I could get. To achieve consistent accuracy, we were taught how to achieve our battlesight zero (BZO). Perhaps the most important concept we learned was the elevation and windage settings on our rifles that would allow us to accurately fire our weapons under ideal conditions. As we encountered external challenges that would affect our accuracy, such as weather and wind conditions, we would be able to make quick adjustments to improve our aim.

Determining a proper battlesight zero is crucial in combat as it allows Marines to engage an enemy threat without spending life-saving time to continually adjust the elevation of their iron sight posts. As a business leader, your ability to achieve consistent accuracy, despite any possible threat or exterior condition, is vital for your survival.

It should come as no surprise that the Corps provides each Marine with strategies, techniques, and resources to qualify as a rifleman. Every Marine is issued a Data Book; a journal of every shot fired. This allows for course-corrections (accountability), by making necessary adjustments to the rifle.

Weapon maintenance is held in the highest regard. Marines field strip their rifles and do a thorough cleaning, which ensures that their weapons work properly and affords them the greatest chances for accuracy and survival, when it is needed the most. When your life is on the line, you embrace every opportunity you can to exceed expectations. Because livelihoods are at stake, it behooves business leaders to have this same focus.

SET YOUR SIGHTS ON SUCCESS

Based on the organizational challenges faced by many leaders, such as poor infrastructure, weak corporate culture, and lackluster performance, achieving basic results can often seem like a daunting task. With overwhelming circumstances, the idea of exceeding possibilities might not even appear as a distant blip on the radar for most.

Regardless of their struggles, leaders are judged on their ability to identify and achieve the necessary results to move their organizations forward and upward. Anything less can paralyze an organization, destroy momentum, and create uncertainty among team members. Failure is not an option for a leader.

While an abundance of leadership "training" programs and "expert" advice is available for today's aspiring leaders, predictable results still elude many organizations. Hitting the target might often seem impossible, especially when leaders fail to be developed and are not able to fluently speak

"Leadership." The Elite Leadership System (ELS) allows you to do more than hit the target with great accuracy; it positions your entire team to exceed possibilities.

Leadership Link Leaders who can exceed possibilities, uniquely position themselves for greater opportunities.

Every leader must focus on their target. What are you aiming for? It is critical to identify the possibilities you need to exceed, then ask yourself, "What am I doing to ensure that my accuracy stays on par with my desired results?" Much like a Marine setting his BZO, you will set your Leadership Sight Zero (LZO). Your LZO will help to improve your focus, your accuracy, and your results. Starting this process is exciting and surprisingly simple.

ADJUST YOUR SIGHTS

The need for strong leaders has never been greater, but the number of leaders able to achieve sustainable results has never been lower. Leaders are rarely issued magic wands, a crystal ball, or a book of spells. Yet daily, they are expected to pull off the impossible. They seldom receive much guidance, and the expectations placed upon them often feel insurmountable.

When I began to assume leadership duties at the post-production company, I was aware of the internal components we needed to address and improve. Our culture required an overhaul, a better workflow was necessary, and a more aggressive sales strategy was paramount. The owner of the company expressed the goal of doubling our sales revenue, which was no small task, especially in a highly technical industry that was evolving rapidly.

I did more than merely set out to double our sales results. I was determined to exceed possibilities by striving for more. My goal was not without merit. I analyzed our current industry environment, assessed our competition, and determined that our internal weaknesses could become significant strengths.

The available new business was out there, so I created a solid *plan*, built a *leadership* team to carry out the plan, and consistently stretched the *vision* of everyone in our organization.

What were my results? Within eighteen months, I had been promoted from an entry-level scheduler to the operations supervisor, to the facility manager, and finally to the vice president of the entire company. But these promotions did not occur solely because we achieved our desired results. They happened because we exceeded possibilities.

As the VP, I actively supported the team and watched our annual revenue elevate to over 300 percent. Because of increased efficiencies, we also experienced greater profit margins and higher levels of customer satisfaction. The opportunities for growth opened up for everyone on our team. Personal and professional development ushered in promotions and raises for many team members.

This level of growth did not happen by accident, nor did it happen by merely striving for better results. It occurred because I systematically applied key strategies that allowed me to set my Leadership Sight Zero (LZO), and consistently exceed possibilities.

The Key Strategies to Set Your LZO and Exceed Possibilities:

- Have a plan
- Build leaders
- Become a visionary leader

As a leader, I have always understood that my core responsibility was to achieve the results set forth by the organization. As a successful leader, I continue to establish my Leadership Sight Zero and focus on more than the results. I set my sights on exceeding possibilities and making the necessary adjustments to hit the target – to get the Bullseye.

Setting your LZO will make the impossible inevitable. At the end of the day, leaders are judged predominantly on what they have achieved. Good intentions and a great personality only go so far. Having a strategic plan, building strong leaders, and becoming a visionary leader, will do much more than enable you to achieve results – you and your team will experience the life-changing feeling of exceeding possibilities.

Chapter 10

Have a Plan

Stop Winging It.

Today is going to be a great day. You can just feel it. You leave your house, slightly ahead of schedule and confidently step up to your car. You take your keys out of your pocket and open the door, already envisioning the extraordinary results that lay ahead. Ready to seize the day, you put your key into the ignition and give it a turn. Nothing happens. Not a sputter; not a clank. You try again. Nothing happens. You try once more. Again, the engine fails to start, and your excitement about the day has fizzled.

There are few things as frustrating as a car that will not start, especially when you need to get somewhere important. With the anticipation of guiding their teams to greater results, every leader needs to go somewhere important, too. Unfortunately, most never take the first step on the journey to elite performance - not because they lack the skills, but because they lack a plan.

Without a plan, leaders are often rendered immobile, unable to move their teams and their organizations in the right direction. Deciding to be greater is a wise choice, but good motives will not take leaders to where they need to go. They need a roadmap to make their desires a reality.

When I ask business leaders to show me their plan for achieving success, my question is usually followed by an awkward silence as they explain why they do not have a formal plan for all of the great aspirations they described to me just moments earlier. I inquire about anything they might have put together to grow their organization; a basic outline or even some notes. Again, nothing. Their plan usually exists only in their minds.

Having the thoughts *of* success is far different than having a plan *for* success. Like a car that won't start, a leader without a plan remains parked. Those who are not able to support the achievement of sustained growth are often left frustrated and discouraged. Turning the key and failing to achieve results can be devastating, but your trip to success does not need to stay like that.

I rarely have difficulty finding leaders with high hopes. But finding leaders who have mapped out the strategic and tactical components necessary for extraordinary results is a different story. Too many leaders excitedly embark on their expedition, hoping to arrive at new and exciting destinations with little to no planning - no clear pathway for success.

Leadership Link Have a plan, so you and your team are never left just "winging-it."

THE IMPORTANCE OF A PLAN

I firmly believe that most leaders intend to succeed, and they genuinely want to win. But even good intentions can yield bad results when we fail to map out our strategy. A plan is one of the greatest tools we have as leaders. But it is often the most underutilized, typically because leaders do not speak the language of *planning*.

I attended film school with the outcome of working in the film business. While I was taught all about "film" (filmmaking), I was never required to attend classes to learn about the "business" side of my new career. Like most other leaders, we learn the "prefix" of our businesses, but rarely learn the *business* aspect of running a business.

- Filmmakers learn about movies

- Doctors learn about medicine

- Attorneys learn about law

- Designers learn about fashion

- Scientists learn about... well, science

Even some of the most highly-educated people, who run businesses, never took business classes. They do not understand how to put together a plan, even though the idea of having a plan makes sense. In my book, *ELEVATE: Take Your Business to the Next Level,* I introduce business leaders to a new way of planning for success, all based on aviation concepts and language.

Your business is an aircraft and was not designed to remain on the airfield of mediocrity – it was designed to elevate to new and exciting levels. Just as every pilot must view their flight plan before taking off, every business pilot must harness the visual power of their *Business Flight Plan.*

LATIN LESSON

VIDERE est CREDERE

Seeing is Believing

Videre est Credere, initially used in a spiritual context, is a phrase first recorded in 1639 to suggest that "only physical or concrete evidence is convincing." According to Cambridge Dictionary: if you see something yourself, you will believe it to exist or be true, despite the fact that it may be unlikely. Perhaps you have goals that seem too big, impossible to accomplish, or unlikely to achieve. Seeing is believing – your goals go into your plan, so they become visible.

Researchers agree that about 75% of our learning is through our vision. According to neuroscientist, Dr. John Medina, "The more visual the input becomes, the more likely it is to be recognized and recalled." Neuroscientists state that between 50%-80% of our brain's processing power is dedicated to seeing and processing our visual sense, which is the key to interacting with the world around us. Our vision trumps all the other senses when it comes to learning.

Visual stimulation helps brain development the most and one study showed that those who used visual presentation tools to convey information were 43%

more successful than those that did not! The bottom line is this: You will be more successful at accomplishing your goals when they are in a plan and your people can see it.

Leadership The more people who can see your plan, the more people can
Link believe in your plan.

IMPROVING YOUR TIME

Just days before graduating from boot camp, the recruits of Platoon 1095 completed their final Physical Fitness Test (PFT). In addition to all the sit-ups and pull-ups, we needed to complete our three-mile run in less than twenty-eight minutes. I am not a runner, so the idea of running three miles was a bit intimidating. The challenge of doing it within such a time frame seemed nearly impossible at the beginning of our training.

I soon discovered that exceeding possibilities was not a suggestion in the Marine Corps. It was part of their plan. The first time our drill instructors took us on a run, we ran less than a mile. But it felt like the full three miles – maybe a little more. I struggled to keep up my pace and was completely winded when we finished the brief run. My only thought was, "If I had difficulty with one mile, how could I possibly do three miles in less than twenty-eight minutes?"

For our transformation into U.S. Marines, our daily training was filled with many challenging objectives. Running was just one of them. Every minute of each day was meticulously *planned* out by our drill instructors, and with our graduation day rapidly approaching, they left nothing to chance. We were not always privy to every detail in their plan, but knowing they had one, raised our belief levels.

Occasionally, we would catch a quick glimpse of their plan. Each drill instructor kept a small index card with him, detailing all the daily activities that would keep us headed in the right direction with our goals. Meticulous planning ensured that we did not miss any of the steps needed for our growth and development, including our ability to complete a three-mile run.

After months of sticking to the plan, I was ready to tackle my running challenge. Crossing the finish line, in the allotted time was another step to becoming one of the few; one of the proud. It would help me to accomplish the goal of becoming a United States Marine.

Checking his stopwatch, Sergeant Hughes yelled out my final time as I crossed the finish line. I did better than run three miles in the required time. I ran three miles in eighteen minutes and fifty seconds. I not only achieved my desired results, but I surpassed my own possibilities. Our leaders did not take their mission lightly, nor did they wing it or merely rely on hope. Leaders in the military have a plan to guarantee the success of their teams.

THE NEED FOR A PLAN

Nearly twelve years after my tour of duty with the Marine Corps ended, I found myself again relying on the power of a plan to achieve results. As a newly promoted leader at the post-production company, it was time to share our annual revenue goal. For our first year, we announced an increase of only 10%. That number was low, based on our potential, and the team's reaction was still less than enthusiastic.

They immediately focused on how busy they already were, and pointed out that we would need more staff, more resources, more everything. Because our current workload seemed difficult to manage, the idea of increasing it seemed impossible. But leaders should always strive for exceeding possibilities, right?

My team's limited belief level would not allow them to see our true potential. I firmly believed we were capable of increasing sales by much more. After a closer look at our missed opportunities, I projected we could achieve at least 20 percent growth in the upcoming year. But if my team failed to even believe we could achieve 10 percent, how could they wrap their heads around the idea of 20 percent?

Before sharing our goal of 10 percent with them, I needed more than mere words of inspiration. I needed something they could see; something that could clarify my vision and remove their excuses. I needed a solid plan. Success might start with vision, but results are achieved only by a team dedicated to following a plan.

Based on the needs of each individual organization, plans can vary drastically in size and scope. Deciding which type of plan will best serve the goals of your organization can often be challenging. Understanding the purpose of specific types of plans will allow you to combine elements from each, customizing a plan that best suits your needs.

Leadership Link Include your team in the creation of your plan and you will increase their desire to support it.

UNDERSTANDING YOUR PLAN

In addition to receiving little to no formal training on the planning process for their businesses, there are also many types of plans a leader can utilize. Choosing the right plan will be critical to accomplishing your goals, engaging your team, and achieving the results your organization needs. So, let's take a quick look at some different types of plans and their main purpose.

Types of Plans

- Business Plan
- Strategic Plan
- Tactical Plan
- Marketing Plan
- Operational Plan
- Financial Plan

Business Plan

Often used for start-up purposes and to provide exit strategies. Business plans are typically used to acquire additional funding from banks and other investors.

Strategic Plan

Involves analyzing new opportunities, competition, and possible challenges. Strategic plans seek to maximize the strengths and minimize the weaknesses of the organization, while determining how to position the team for greater effectiveness.

Tactical Plan

Short-term in nature, these plans focus on developing immediate actionable items that will support any long-term planning. They increase the involvement of mid-level leaders and their team members to improve workflow and customer service.

Marketing Plan

Typically part of the overall business plan, marketing plans focus on the advertising and marketing objectives, and efforts required within specific time frames – usually in one-year intervals.

Operational Plan

Also short-term in nature, operational plans focus on improving the efficiencies and effectiveness of specific departments, as they relate to the overall long-term goals of the organization. They might involve restructuring, especially as it relates to the quality of the staff.

Financial Plan

The elements that determine how an organization will afford to achieve its goals and objectives. Financial plans are typically created after the organizational objectives have been set. Financial plans establish timeframes and lists the staff, resources, equipment, and materials needed to achieve these objectives.

TAKING OFF

I often witness leaders working relentlessly on the "busy work" of their business. They miss out on the opportunity to create a plan that will shift everyone's focus onto the big picture of the organization and the actions necessary for growth. This misguided focus can be one of the biggest mistakes leaders make.

Having the right plan is the first step in exceeding possibilities. While most leaders readily agree that having a plan is valuable, few dedicate the time, resources, and investment to gain the unparalleled return that this powerful tool yields. A plan provides us with three significant benefits that impact the belief levels of our teams.

The Three Benefits of Having a Plan:

1. Increases Buy-In

2. Opens New Opportunities

3. Moves the Future Closer

To experience the benefits of a plan, leaders must be fully committed to the detailed development, implementation, and continuous course-correction needed to achieve high-level results. It always pays to have a plan.

Increases Buy-In

The high aspirations of leaders do not always have the desired effect on their teams. Powerful goals, prioritized objectives, and important tasks might fail to gain momentum when the team is not completely aligned with the projected results. Because most people associate growth with additional workload, they are often hesitant to voluntarily take on new projects.

The process of planning increases the buy-in from the team by outlining the organization's mission with a detailed roadmap for success, allowing team members to see the direction and the destination. If possible, involve your team in the development of the plan, or at least specific components. Involvement fosters additional buy-in.

Buy-in increases as leaders articulate each team member's connection with the plan and what will be expected of them. Planning makes your team stronger by tapping into their strengths and providing the necessary training to minimize their weaknesses.

Leadership Link Invest time with your team and consistently share the progress being made on the plan.

Opens New Opportunities

Many leaders are often charismatic, inspirational, and influential. Team members might be captivated by their personalities, but not truly understand their directions. Unfortunately, neither do those leaders. When leaders fail to plan, more is lost than just the desired results.

- Planning opens new opportunities that would have otherwise, never been imaginable.

- Planning enables leaders to do more than just share their vision; it enables people to bring their A-game to the table.

- Planning promotes high-level collaboration, which allows people to hone their skills and maximize their resources.

- Planning gets people involved in discovering solutions, which is when the real magic starts.

- Planning allows an organization to be bigger than the collective efforts of just one person, by ushering in additional ideas for growth. New ideas create new opportunities that allow the plan to achieve results faster and more effectively.

Leadership Link Encourage team members to discuss specific components of the plan and support their collaborative efforts. New opportunities will open.

Moves the Future Closer

Working with many business leaders on their plans, I have found a bit of reluctance when initially setting time frames for key long-term goals. Understandably, most leaders do not want to overpromise and underdeliver. Planning increases efficiencies and effectiveness, taking into account all of the aspects of an organization and how they relate to one another.

Looking at the business in this manner encourages the elimination of the components that do not support the greater vision. The benefits of planning help leaders to position themselves to move future dates closer as more short-term goals are accomplished, usually ahead of schedule. This allows for the creation of a long-term vision, even if you cannot fully see it in its final view.

Dream a little and *think great*, projecting out at least a few years. Try focusing on where you need to be in five years; not just what appears to be realistic, but what you desire. Set your sights on higher levels of achievement and you will allow your organization to move in new directions. This will also allow you to be cognizant of the necessary steps to get there.

Leadership Link A plan allows your team to participate in the growth and success of your organization.

CHOOSING YOUR PLAN

While each type of plan provides a variety of benefits and accomplishes specific outcomes, only one has been engineered for you and your team to consistently elevate to new levels. The *Flight Plan* is a customized tool for leaders to become Business Aviators and achieve balance in their leadership role while positioning their business to rise to the highest levels of success, growth, and engagement.

The *Flight Plan* is an integral part of our Business Elevation System (BES). It provides a shared-language, the tools required for take-off, and three distinct benefits to Business Aviators and their teams.

The Three Benefits of a Flight Plan:

1. A visual representation of your goals

2. A detailed account of the steps for success

3. A constant confirmation of your commitment

Because every organization is at different stages in their development, your Flight Plan will encapsulate where your business is and where it needs to go. It will provide your Flight Crew with the guidance systems to get there. Some organizations require more attention to operational excellence, while others need additional sales training. Some need to improve their workflow, while others need to expand their product line.

Regardless of where your organization currently rests, your *Flight Plan* will begin to move your organization forward by teaching you and your people the four components required to successfully elevate business to new and exciting flight levels.

The Four Forces of Business Elevation:

1. Flight Plan Creation

2. Aircrew Development

3. Tactical Maneuvers

4. Ascension Enhancement

A *Flight Plan* is much like the blueprints to a home. Can you imagine building a house without blueprints? Would you feel safe moving your family in if the contractors were merely winging it? Building a business is no different. Your Flight Plan will provide safety, security and stability to your entire team by uniquely combining the critical components required to harness the *Four Forces of Business Elevation*.

The Critical Components of a Flight Plan:

Business Assessment

Before attempting to take-off, analyze the stability of your business, your leaders, and your team.

Strengths

Identify the power sources of your business. These areas will move you forward and provide *lift*.

Weaknesses

Identify the areas that need to be improved. These are the elements that currently provide *drag* to your business aircraft and hinder your flight.

Opportunities

List all the amazing opportunities that your business is currently missing: new markets, increased revenue share, and new services.

Identity

Combine everything that forms your team identity: mission statement, vision statement, core values, taglines, and mottos. The stronger the identity, the stronger the commitment.

Flight Levels

Identify all the goals that need to be accomplished in the next five years, three years, and one year. Next, focus on the goals that need to be accomplished in the next 90 days.

FOD (Foreign Object Debris)

You and your team will identify anything that should not be on your runway; anything that will prohibit your aircraft from taking off, and anything that will cause it to fail to achieve elevation.

There is much more that goes into every *Flight Plan*. Business Aviators will work together to remove FOD with the help of the FOD Prevention Plan. They will break down each Flight Level, establishing the purpose of each goal and assigning key team members to accomplish it. Each goal will also be assigned a Crew Chief - one person in charge and responsible, not to do all the work, but rather to make sure it all happens.

Complete with a quarterly *Post-Flight Checklist*, you and your team will be able to take-off, elevate, and stay on course. For more information about the *Business Elevation System (BES)* and how to create your *Flight Plan*, check out my book, *ELEVATE: Take Your Business to the Next Level*. Enroll your team in our *Business Flight School* and a Think GREAT facilitator will guide your team through the *BES*.

Leadership Link Your Flight Plan will do much more than elevate your business; it will elevate engagement.

STARTING YOUR PLAN

While there are common planning challenges shared among nearly every leader, I believe there is one primary hurdle we have all faced as we begin to create a plan for a greater future. Most leaders simply do not know where to start. How do you begin to develop a plan that encompasses so much? You can start by utilizing two simple tools – a napkin and a pen.

I believe that these are the most significant planning resources ever created. In 2008, I wrote *Think GREAT* on a napkin and now I travel across the country to teach personal and professional development strategies. You are reading this book because of that napkin and pen. Imagine what you could do with these same tools.

While at lunch to discuss the completion of Pixar's animated film, *Toy Story*, director, John Lasseter, and three writers asked the question, "What's next?" Their question led to some sketches on the back of a napkin, which began the planning process for some of Pixar's next films: *A Bug's Life, Monsters, Inc., Finding Nemo,* and *Wall-E.*

These four films grossed nearly $2.5 billion in ticket sales alone, not including additional merchandise such as toys and DVDs. This does not include any sequels to these huge hits. Finding Dory and Toy Story 3 both had ticket sales in excess of $1 billion each. Great things can be accomplished when you take the time to formulate your plan. What could you accomplish if you took the time to start yours?

As the Operations Supervisor at the media company, I was not an expert in plan-writing. The first plan I initially constructed probably looked like some amateur sketches, but it became the foundation of our organization. If it was not in our plan, we did not waste time on it. If it was in our plan, we invested everything we had into achieving it.

With the help and support of my entire team, we tweaked, enhanced, and updated our plan at least a dozen times during our growth phase. This plan allowed us to exceed the 10 percent growth goal for our first year. We hit 23.99 percent sales growth. The second year we shot for 25 percent growth and landed at 65 percent sales growth, positioning us to eventually increase our annual sales revenue by over 300 percent.

The evolution and refinement of the planning process is what I now share as The *Business Elevation System.* The *Flight Plan* has a proven history of success. Will you use it to elevate your future? Start by jotting a few lines on the back of a napkin, perhaps with the collaborative insights from some of your team members. Allow the excitement of ideas to flow as you collaborate and discover innovative ways to ascend.

Fortunately, your plan does not need to be one-hundred percent complete to start enjoying the rewards. The process of starting a plan often unifies members of your team, especially as you include them in the development process.

SLOW DOWN TO SPEED UP

By not investing the necessary time to develop a plan for growth, leaders often find themselves resolving ongoing issues and fighting fires, rather than moving their organizations along the pathway to success. Planning holds leaders accountable and allows them to become proactive with the priority goals required for new levels of elevation.

Take the time to plan. Slow down so you and your team can speed up - the right way. Plans allow us to course-correct, which is inherently important, especially with the many competing distractions and challenges we face in our daily lives.

Most leaders want to achieve greater results; they want to exceed possibilities. But they have no roadmap to guide themselves and their teams in the right direction. Avoid unnecessary turmoil by mapping out your destination ahead of time. Stay a step ahead of your competition and position your organization for a truly dynamic flight.

You do not need to be an expert in writing plans to create a plan that will help you to exceed possibilities. Planning is about developing a better understanding of your organization. In its most simplistic form, it answers three key questions.

1. Where are you now?

2. Where do you need to go?

3. How do you get there?

The initial plan I developed at the media company was far from perfect, but it enabled progress by unifying our team with clarity and purpose. To the best of our abilities, we projected out our next three to five years. With our end goal in mind, we launched our plan and focused our efforts intensely on the first ninety days. We used this block of time as an opportunity to harness our skills and course-correct our progress.

Because a successful plan requires the efforts of your entire team, make the commitment to *Build Leaders* at every level.

LEADERSHIP STEPS

HAVE A PLAN

Elite Leadership Step – Assemble the Aviators

- As you begin the exciting process of creating your plan, you will need to identify your Business Aviators – the people in charge of developing and carrying out the detailed plan. They are typically your key leaders who have a track record for hitting the target and getting things done. Remember, "Earned, never given," when choosing your crew.

Additional Steps

- **Opportunity:** Begin by identifying all the possibilities available for your business. Topping your list may be opportunities such as new clients, new markets, and increasing sales with existing customers. Assess the scope of the available "Pie" and what your slice looks like – your plan will detail how to carve it out.

- **Challenges:** With your Aviators, identify the perceived challenges of the planning process. Perhaps a lack of time, lack of skills, and a lack of resources could hinder the forward momentum. Perhaps the team is not aligned, or worse yet, the leaders are not operating in alignment. Next, read *ELEVATE*, to discover the techniques to remove your challenges.

- **Long-Term:** In addition to working your short-term goals into your plan, your Flight Crew must identify the long-term strategic goals that will elevate your business into the future. These are critical as they provide inspiring steps toward the vision of the organization.

Chapter 11

Build Leaders

Developing GREAT Leaders is Your Business.

Putting together a plan for growth in your organization is an enlightening and rewarding experience. But the implementation, execution, and success of that plan will rest on the shoulders of every leader. How important is it to build leaders at every level? A strong leader can transform a weak plan into victory, while a weak leader may minimize the impact of even the strongest plan.

Developing effective leadership, at all levels across an organization, will return significant value. Planting leadership seeds and building leaders is the greatest security system you can install within your business. In addition to supporting your plan, leaders also help protect your organization from the constant attack of your competition. New products, lower prices, and aggressive marketing campaigns are just a few ways your rivals can strike.

But the most fatal blow a business can suffer comes as members of its team are hired away for the hopes of a better opportunity. But competitors rarely go after your under-performers. They set their sights on those who deliver results; those who can exceed possibilities. Strong leaders are under constant observation and you can be certain that your competition is sizing them up and determining how your people can support their plan.

Losing a leader to a competitor is a highly damaging mistake. It is estimated that this can cost an organization two to three times the annual salary of that leader if he or she decides to hang their hat with your rival. When you factor in all the time, resources, and investments that went into the training required to get them up to speed, it can be catastrophic to see them leave for a new journey.

The impact of losing a leader can be devastating to your team, affecting workload, morale, and customer satisfaction. The departure of a key leader can send a negative ripple effect throughout your organization and to your customers, dramatically hindering your efforts for growth. One of the greatest aspects of building leaders is that it increases their desire to stay.

Leadership Build your leaders so you can retain them.
Link

Elite leaders do not leave their jobs solely because they can make more money elsewhere. They typically leave because they feel underappreciated, underchallenged, or they perceive there is greater opportunity for growth elsewhere. Before your leaders leave to rebuild themselves elsewhere, invest the time necessary to build them while they are still on your team. But to truly exceed possibilities, teach them how to build their people as leaders.

THE IMPORTANCE OF BUILDING LEADERS

I am amazed at the lack of leadership development that occurs in most businesses, especially when leaders rank its importance at astronomically high. Why is there such a disconnect between the desire for leadership development and the implementation of it? The answer is quite simple. Just as most leaders have no formal education in strategic planning, they usually also lack any formal development in the *art* of leading.

Plainly stated, they are not fluent in leadership, therefore, they do not speak it. When leadership is not spoken, how can it grow? Titles of leadership are assigned, sometimes to appease people. Positions are appointed, but often lack purpose. "Leadership Meetings" are conducted, but rarely is the word *leader* ever mentioned. These gatherings are more ceremonious than purpose-driven and tend to be void of discussions about traits, principles, or anything else that remotely resembles leadership.

Business leaders are typically fluent in their business language, speaking with great authority on their products and services, but are again, speechless when it comes to the *artform* known as leadership. I know what you're thinking, "He's mentioned that leadership is an *artform* a few times now, so where is he going with it?" Great question!

The Army and the Marine Corps may have their differences, but they both share a similar perspective on leadership. The Army's *Leadership Handbook* states, "Leadership is paramount to our profession. It is integral to our institutional success today and tomorrow... You will face difficult decisions and dilemmas. This is all part of the process of learning the *art* of leadership."

The Marine Corps' *Essential Subjects Handbook*, states that "Leadership has passed from Marine to Marine since the founding of the Corps (1775). It is the *art* of influencing and directing men and women to accomplish the mission of keeping our country free."

Leadership Link Because leadership is truly an artform, then our canvas is our people.

When leadership is this important to an organization, they do not hope it happens, they continuously develop their people to ensure that it happens. The Marines mention passing leadership down from Marine to Marine because that's precisely what they do. Within the first week of boot camp, I was handed on olive-drab satchel and the handbook containing all the "Practical Knowledge" we needed to learn to graduate from boot camp.

As the Prac (pronounced Prak) Recruit for Platoon 1095, I was instructed to teach the subjects in the book, every time there was an opportunity. When we lined up to enter the chow hall, I broke out the book and taught. When we were cleaning our rifles, I opened the satchel and instructed. I covered everything from Marine Corps history to rank structure and topics ranging from combat hand signals to, yes, you guessed it, leadership.

LATIN LESSON

AEDIFICARE DUCTUS

To Build Leaders

As the Roman philosopher Seneca said, "While we teach, we learn." Remember the *Latin Lesson* from Chapter 8: *Docendo Discimus* (Learning by teaching)? Imagine the impact when your team begins to not only be cultivated as leaders, but they begin to teach leadership to develop their team members. To build leaders we must teach leadership, passing it from one team member to the next, honing our skills in the process.

Boot camp consisted of three phases, each requiring us to pass a test on our knowledge before moving to the next level of training. The night before each test, I would stay up, into the early morning hours, to study with my fellow recruits. I did not want anyone to fail a test and be unable to move forward. It felt like cramming for a test in high school, but the rewards were significant.

The more I taught leadership to my fellow recruits, the more I understood its deeper meaning. The more I shared the fourteen traits, the more I grew. The more I educated my platoon on the eleven principles, the more I developed. The more I discussed leadership, the more I sharpened my leadership blade, which is critically important because I have discovered that every leader performs like one of two specific *leadership* blades. Which one are you?

1. Leadership Butter Knife

2. Leadership Katana Sword

Leadership butter knives typically hold the position of a leader but do little to develop themselves or the others around them – they never sharpen their leadership skills. Leaders who perform as butter knives seldom do little more than spread things around: workload, responsibilities, and sometimes, even negativity. In a utensil drawer, butter knives do serve a purpose but are limited in what they can do. When one goes missing, they are seldom missed and easily replaced.

Then there is the Leadership Katana Sword (does not fit in a drawer). Used by the ancient samurai of Japan, this blade is unique – masterfully forged in a kiln. Placed into the intense heat of the fire (1,600° F), the metal transforms. It becomes soft, moldable, and ultimately stronger. While still hot, the sword is pounded to help it take its shape. Great pride is taken with this forged metal. The Katana is synonymous with honor, discipline, and precision.

It is not uncommon to see a Katana blade proudly mounted on the mantle above a fireplace. I have yet to see a butter knife mounted – anywhere. Great swords, like great leaders, go back into the fire and receive their fair share of transformational forging. Leaders who perform like Katana swords cut right through the issues and ensure the job gets done right. They are a symbol of excellence to their teams.

Leadership Link Always be a "sharp" leader – a symbol of what it means to be a leader in your organization.

PRACTICE, PRACTICE, PRACTICE

Just as samurai must relentlessly practice in order to effectively use his weapon, leaders must also practice leading. In order to compete in the Olympics, athletes must regularly practice their sport. But to win the gold medal, they must be all in – they must live their sport. With twenty-eight Olympic medals around his neck, twenty-three of which are gold, it is fair to say that Michael Phelps practiced swimming with great intensity and focus.

Unfortunately, most leaders only dip their big toe into the leadership pool, neglecting practice for the busy work that consumes their day. Their "IN's" keep them out of the pool. Just as Michael Phelps trained with purpose, leaders must take the same approach and teach their people to also practice the *art* of leading.

When we practice leadership, we are honing our skills while simultaneously making an impact in everyone on our team. Every organization is built upon the leadership capabilities of their people. Weak leaders simply cannot support strong growth – they cannot support the plan for a greater future.

As the old saying goes, "People truly are your greatest asset." But they can be your greatest weakness when left undeveloped. Building them up as leaders might provide your organization with the only real competitive advantage in business. But most organizations neglect tapping into the true potential of their team.

Constrained by antiquated management processes and a dismal culture, most leaders merely uphold out-of-touch policies, procedures, and best practices. They fail to deliver the results that are possible because they never "practice" the craft of leadership. Anyone can call themselves an expert marksman by showing up at the rifle range, wearing the appropriate attire, and brandishing a weapon. While you might appear to be a rifleman, looks only go so far. Eventually, people will evaluate you on your results.

As a U.S. Marine, being proficient with our weapons required intense focus, dedication, and countless hours of repetitive practice. If we failed to fine-tune our abilities, we would fail to produce the desired results. Just showing up in our camouflage uniforms was not good enough when the target was in sight. Many leaders show up and look the part. But unless they practice leadership, on a regular basis, their aim will be off, and they will completely miss the target – every time.

People are not born as leaders. That way of thinking has long since passed. Like all things, leadership is a learned behavior. It can and should be taught at all levels in an organization. Once reserved for the select few who hold the top positions, leadership development is proven to benefit the entire team – a secret the military has known for hundreds of years.

I once trained over 100 people at the annual workshop for the National Association of Health Unit Coordinators. Representatives from all over the country attended my session. While most were not in a leadership position, I was asked to train them on the benefits of applying leadership skills to their current positions.

I discussed communication, goal-setting, and the 14 Leadership Traits of the Marine Corps. The feedback was overwhelmingly positive. Leadership development, to people who were not in leadership roles, empowered them far more than any of the training they received. They focused on becoming better team players, helping to build stronger cultures, and achieving greater results. How would you like that to happen in your business? It takes practice!

Leadership Link Leadership is not intended to be a lonely position. Develop your entire team as leaders so you are not on a leadership island by yourself.

PRACTICE LEADERSHIP

Exceeding possibilities is one of the elite purposes of all leaders, so it is in your best interest to develop the leadership skills of those around you. Building leaders will help you to achieve results and lift your entire team to new levels of professionalism. In addition to the intense focus placed on Marines to become proficient with their weapons, their combat skills, and their other occupational specialties, Marines consistently practice leadership.

Building up leaders within the ranks of the Corps is not something that might happen, but rather it is something that demands the highest level of constant attention and focus to guarantee that it happens. To effectively practice leadership and build all leaders on your team, focus on three key areas.

How to Effectively Practice Leadership and Build Leaders:

- Identify Leadership Potential
- Create Leadership Activities
- Transfer Leadership Authority

Identify Leadership Potential

Leadership does not have to be a lonely position. Identify and develop current managers and high-performing team members to competently share your responsibilities as a leader. Identifying someone as a possible leader is one of the greatest compliments you can give. As a leader of leaders, I always kept my eyes and ears open to the signs of future leadership at the media company.

I took opportunities to talk to my staff, assessing their desire to rise up within our organization and contribute to the success of our plan. Within your ranks, identify each current leader and team member who possesses the leadership skills, or the raw potential, to make a greater impact within your company.

Acknowledging the leadership potential within your team serves many purposes. In addition to allowing for internal growth, it simultaneously guards against unnecessary turnover. It also brings forth more promotions and fosters an environment of dedication and loyalty.

From a fiscal perspective, it is often less expensive to retain and develop your own talent, rather than hiring from other sources. If your team feels leaders are only hired from outside of your organization, they might look outside of your organization for new opportunities. Allow your team to see opportunities for growth within your company.

During our push toward 300 percent revenue growth, the vast majority of our leadership team started their journey with us in entry-level positions, including myself. I was given the opportunity to make an impact and I made a sizable one. What could your team do if you identified their leadership potential and built them up as leaders?

Create Leadership Activities

Most organizations have people in leadership positions but offer very few opportunities for them to hone their abilities – to flex their leadership muscles. Athletes must participate in athletic activities to hone their skills. Their coaches provide unlimited opportunities for them to become better, stronger, faster.

Strength training, team practices, one-on-one coaching, and scrimmaging against other teams all help to develop stronger skills.

Leaders need to participate in leadership activities to fine-tune their skills. Your goal is to build the leaders on your team above their basic duties and give them a broader set of responsibilities to support the plan for the organization. I created activities that went far beyond training on the philosophies of leadership. Our activities focused on building our leaders; involving them in actual examples of what to do and what not to do.

To develop my leaders, I held actual leadership meetings, providing them with ways to learn, to share, and to grow with their fellow leaders. We read leadership books, discussed our most significant take-aways, and applied the techniques to our day-to-day encounters with our people. Our leadership meetings focused exclusively on leadership topics, dialogue, and scenarios.

In addition to setting high standards for their personal performance, I was involved in the hands-on cultivation with each of them, taking specific case studies and analyzing ways each leader could improve their results. We identified ways to improve communication with other leaders, other team members, and with customers and vendors.

We addressed techniques that worked and did not work. We sought out solutions that would enable everyone to become the epitome of leadership; to be a shining example to the team of what it meant to be a leader in our organization. We taught them how to be the beacon of hope, especially during any challenging circumstances.

Perhaps one of the greatest activities you can orchestrate is the personal interaction among your leaders. Understanding the need to connect my leaders on levels deeper than their job descriptions, we often met off-site for coffees, lunches, and dinners. We even conducted some of our meetings at unique locations and sometimes, at unconventional times.

To unveil our updated plan for the third quarter, I called an optional meeting for our leadership team. The location was on the top floor of the Huntley Hotel, in Santa Monica, California. The meeting was set for

Friday evening at their restaurant, The Penthouse. The time was set for midnight. Yes, our meeting began as the clock struck twelve. No one was required to attend.

Yet all ten members of our leadership team enthusiastically attended and participated. We stayed for nearly three hours. While we discussed the plan, we also discussed our personal goals. We learned much more about each other during this unique activity than we had over the past years of working together. A stronger bond was created between our leadership team and we further unified our environment. Activities like this provided some of our greatest moments of development.

Transfer Leadership Authority

The authority of a leader provides the boundaries for course-correcting their team members and making other important decisions. Like currency, possessing the proper authority allows a leader to fully invest in their team by combining praising, reprimanding, and influencing. Failing to transfer the proper amount of authority creates a "broke" leader, incapable of making the impact necessary to support the organization's plan for growth.

The failure to transfer the proper authority to a leader, may be the most damaging mistake. A leader with no authority is nothing more than a team member who stands higher on the "corporate ladder" but can accomplish little more. Leadership positions should not be given as status symbols or ways to appease long-term employees.

When we delegate with a purpose (Chapter 5), we transfer the authority required for our team members to make the decisions necessary to move a *task* forward. But when we build leaders and delegate the responsibility of leading, we must transfer the authority required to move the *people* forward.

When a leader earns a promotion, the transference of authority must coincide with the new position. When authority fails to transfer, it is typically due to a lack of understanding its significance. So, let's take a closer look at the definition.

authority

noun

- The power to make decisions.
- The right to direct someone or something.
- The ability to settle issues.
- An accepted source of information.

When a leader is afraid to give control, because they fear losing it, they have defined it incorrectly. Transferring authority is much more than just handing over control. It is transitioning the ability to perform like a leader; the authority to make the decisions required for success – even to make the tough decisions.

Leadership Link Leadership authority is not best used by holding onto it. It is most effective when shared between leaders.

A leadership role is a huge responsibility to fulfill, for the person in the new position as well as the person who provided the opportunity. Unfortunately, most new leaders are not allowed to exercise the full authority of their positions. Existing leaders, who hold onto the reigns of authority, rather than transitioning them to their leaders, often lack the trust needed to make the transfer. That is specifically why leadership must be earned, never given.

By identifying team members with leadership potential and including them in leadership activities, you can successfully transfer specified levels of authority that will allow them to fully support you and your plan. When a leader has little-to-no authority, it sends a negative message to the entire team, completely negating the new leadership position the person had earned.

Invest the necessary time with your leaders to develop them, coach them, and mentor them. Assess their capabilities with small levels of authority, and work together to increase their ability to take on greater challenges. A leadership promotion is not complete until an understanding of their authority has been clearly established – to the leader and to the team.

Leadership With the proper amount of authority, every leader is a weapon
Link of mass achievement!

BECOMING A LEADER OF LEADERS

Within my first six months of serving in the Marine Corps, I was promoted from Private to Private First Class. I was now a rank higher and essentially a leader of junior Marines, and still only eighteen years old. To effectively build leaders, the Marine Corps emphasized extensive leadership programs to all of its Marines. The Corps did not offer one single management course. Everything was built upon leadership development, not leadership training.

As your leadership team grows, your focus should be on the personal development of each member of the team. A quick word of advice: do not attempt to manage your leaders. Become a leader of leaders, taking every possible opportunity to grow your people.

Leadership development is an ongoing journey. As long as you have leaders on your team, your duty as their leader is never finished. Because many leaders struggle with their own skills, they wonder how they can effectively lead other leaders. Having leaders report to me always keeps me focused on increasing my own personal performance – sharpening my leadership blade.

I have always felt that significant results start in an organization when the next wave of leaders rise up to support the senior leadership team. The problem is that most leaders do not identify and cultivate this important line of leadership.

The next wave of leaders has their fingers on the pulse; they know what does and does not work. They know who works and who does not. They are your liaison to the team, and it is your objective to connect with them,

BUILD LEADERS | 185

lead them, and teach them how to properly lead their teams. To become an effective leader of leaders requires you to show up every day with the highest levels of excellence.

To Become a Leader of Leaders:

- Lead by Example
- Invest the Time
- Provide the Feedback

Being a leader is an incredibly rewarding journey. But developing other leaders has always been my greatest pleasure.

Lead by Example

As a leader, all eyes are on you. Your team analyzes your behavior and critiques your performance. As a leader of leaders, everything intensifies. You are under the microscope 24/7. Your actions, patterns, and habits will be duplicated by your team. Setting the example is the best way to ensure that you stay on track, and your people have the proper model to emulate.

Many leaders mistakenly think the people working for them are already "set in their ways," and do not have the ability to change, to adapt, to improve. Nothing could be farther from the truth. I have seen many old dogs learn new tricks. It's not the limitations of the dog, but rather the limiting belief level of its trainer that minimizes performance.

Leadership Link Leading by example is a 24/7 commitment.

I have worked with leaders who pointed out the old dinosaurs on their teams, or the top performers who are negative and stuck doing things "the old way." As these leaders were taught how to lead by example and consistently do the right things, even their "problem children" become star students.

Leading by example makes complete sense, but most leaders fail to do it. The first step is to leave our egos outside – yes, get them OUT. It is not about being right; it is about doing right. Do not believe for a second that people do not need you as an example. They absolutely do. Your leaders look to you for the right and wrong ways to do things. Make the choice to lead by example and do the right things.

Set the right example at all times.

Invest the Time

Many senior leaders feel they do not have the time to develop their leaders. Assuming that they will understand how to lead by observation alone is a critical mistake. Take the time to discuss their struggles and their challenges. They certainly will have them and ignoring them only makes matters worse.

Investing the time with your leaders to discover solutions is time well spent. Slowing down and spending this critical time with your people will help everyone to speed up and achieve greater results. While leadership meetings are a great way to encourage leaders to share their thoughts among their peers, I have always found that one-on-one time with my team was worth every minute, especially off-site.

In these relaxed, casual settings, I was able to connect on a deeper level with them. Understanding your leaders is necessary and developing empathy is critical. I not only listened to their struggles, but I also shared mine. It is not necessary to make your leaders think you are flawless – let your guard down and be human. When they know you are faced with challenges, and understand how you resolve them, a deeper level of respect and development occurs.

Invest the time necessary to discuss the nuances of their environments; their team members' personalities, their working relationships with other leaders, and their ideas about the plan for growth. Leaders need an outlet for their thoughts. Being that outlet will pay off for you, for them, and for your entire organization.

Provide the Feedback

Leaders do not want to fail. Unfortunately, most do not realize they are heading down the wrong path until something goes wrong. Backing up from a mistake can be costly and timely and it can also lead to frustrations among your leaders. While we can always learn much from our mistakes, proper guidance minimizes the unnecessary errors we may encounter.

Have you ever watched little kids bowl? No bowler exhibits the raw excitement and energy like these youngsters do as their ball rolls down the lane. How long would that excitement last if their ball consistently went into the gutter? Eventually, they would give up, never experiencing the feeling of knocking down the pins directly in front of them.

Before their skills are sharpened, these young bowlers enjoy the rush of adrenalin as they consistently knock down the pins, with the help of well-placed bumper rails. Your leaders often need your guidance while they are developing their skills. Like the bumper rails on a bowling lane, your regular feedback helps to keep them on target.

Never assume your leaders are already qualified to strike down all the pins on their own. Every leader needs guidance, strategies, and techniques to achieve better results with their team members. Standing by and watching their ball go into the gutter is not an adequate way to build leaders. Eventually they will seek out coaching elsewhere. Be their first option by providing frequent performance evaluations with impactful suggestions for growth.

Leadership Link Leaders need coaching and guidance for their leadership actions.

Performance evaluations might not always feel comfortable but being a leader of leaders is not about staying in your comfort zone. It is about building leaders and providing them with the support they need for success. Frequent evaluations will help you to catch issues early and prevent your leaders from experiencing unnecessary turbulence during their flight. Most leaders will not initially ask for help, so you must discover what their needs are until they trust you enough to directly present their challenges to you.

You cannot hastily build leaders, which is why we did not discuss it until this chapter. The first ten chapters are critical to developing a foundation that will allow you to fulfill this responsibility and exceed possibilities. You are now creating a plan that will be carried out by the leaders you are building. One final step remains. You must *Become a Visionary Leader*.

LEADERSHIP STEPS

BUILD LEADERS

Elite Leadership Step – Identify Next Wave Leaders

- The continual development of leaders is vital for success and we should always be looking for the next wave of leaders to carry the torch. With your other leaders, get off-site to identify the people who are showing leadership promise.

  Next, meet with your up-and-coming leaders to share the insights that other leaders have expressed about their potential. This is a powerful way to recognize your people and to begin building them as leaders.

Additional Steps

- **Results:** Using your *Leadership Sight Zero (LZO)*, work with each of your leaders to define the results they need to hit more accurately; more consistently.

- **Practice:** Describe the current activities that your leaders participate in to sharpen their leadership blades: reading and sharing leadership books, attending and conducting "leadership" meetings, supporting the plan, and getting off-site to develop a deeper understanding of their people.

- **Evaluations:** To grow as leaders, we all need to evaluate our performance and our impact. Use the *Leadership Evaluation* on the next page as a supplement to job reviews with your leaders. Accurately assess their leadership skills and discuss ways to improve.

LEADERSHIP EVALUATION

5 = GREAT Performance   2 = Marginal

4 = Meets Requirements   1 = Unsatisfactory

3 = Needs Improvement

	5	4	3	2	1
Leads by example	☐	☐	☐	☐	☐
Delivers dynamic communication (BEC)	☐	☐	☐	☐	☐
Supports the success of our plan	☐	☐	☐	☐	☐
Empowers others through delegation	☐	☐	☐	☐	☐
Ensures a "Tour Ready" environment	☐	☐	☐	☐	☐
Creates high levels of morale	☐	☐	☐	☐	☐
Raises expectations	☐	☐	☐	☐	☐
Embraces our identity to unify our team	☐	☐	☐	☐	☐
Uses accountability as a partnership tool	☐	☐	☐	☐	☐
Collaborates to discover innovative solutions	☐	☐	☐	☐	☐
Identifies and build leaders	☐	☐	☐	☐	☐
Consistently shares vision	☐	☐	☐	☐	☐
Achieves GREAT results	☐	☐	☐	☐	☐

Chapter 12

Become a Visionary Leader

Bring the Horizon to You.

You have taken significant steps toward achieving consistently positive results in your organization. Having a plan and building leaders are two essential elements to achieving new levels of success. But deep inside, you know you possess the ability to accomplish more; to exceed expectations. To take your results to unbelievable new heights, you must become a visionary leader. I know what some of you may be thinking, "If I'm struggling just to lead, how am I expected to rise to the level of a visionary leader?"

We think of visionary leaders as the architects of new eras – in business and in the world. Much like Gandhi, MLK, and the other leaders mentioned earlier, we characterize them as people with bold and inspiring dreams, wildly brilliant imaginations, and life-changing aspirations. Leaders like George Washington, Rosa Parks, and Steve Jobs would also easily fall into this exclusive category.

We know that visionary leaders do not run from the challenges they face. Instead, they encourage the best from their people to discover solutions while simultaneously unifying them with a shared sense of purpose. They focus on the far-off horizon where a better life awaits, and they rally people to move to that seemingly impossible destination.

Because most of us are not trying to change the world, the idea of becoming a visionary leader not only seems impossible, it seems impractical. Nothing could be farther from the truth. You may not see yourself as visionary, but you should. Every organization needs leaders with vision because every organization has the potential to be greater.

While most leaders are not striving to make an impact on a global scale, many have strong desires to enhance their businesses, their teams, and their livelihoods. It takes vision to see the unlimited possibilities of the future and a visionary leader to guide the team there. To achieve great new results with leadership, you will need to embrace visionary strategies and techniques.

Tackling the toughest challenges in their paths, visionary leaders work with an inspiring passion and loyalty, calling forth the best in every member of their team. They exhibit the highest levels of professionalism and resolve, causing people to have a genuine desire to follow them – enthusiastically. This may seem like a pipe dream but is simpler to achieve than you can imagine.

Leadership Link Visionary leaders inspire people to Exceed Possibilities.

THE IMPORTANCE OF VISION

A Mission Statement is a powerful tool. It is a description of where your business is now and the *mission* that the team must strive to accomplish each day. Not every business utilizes this identity-enhancing tool and even fewer tap into the power of a Vision Statement, which describes what your business will become in the future – the *vision* of where you are going.

A Vision Statement is the first step in the transformation to becoming a visionary leader. More than guiding people to a specified location, visionary leaders imagine new, uncharted destinations, while simultaneously articulating the path for success. But just as many businesses fail to develop their leaders, even more fail to invest the time necessary to unleash the incredible ideas in their minds – their vision.

LATIN LESSON

PHANTASTICUS

Existing in the Imagination

Perhaps the most fun Latin word to say, *Phantasticus* reminds us that vision is something that has not yet been created – it remains in our thoughts, our ideas, and our minds. Beginning in our imagination, we must follow a path to transform vision into reality. As you strive to exceed possibilities by becoming a visionary leader, there are three steps on this unique part of your journey that must consistently happen.

The Three Steps to Transform Vision into Reality:

1. Have Vision

2. Share Vision

3. Stretch Vision

Have Vision

You cannot magically order vision to appear. It exists inside of us and we need to clearly define it in order to fully have it. Vision begins by having glimpses of what is possible in the future. But it needs to become more. Because vision is so critical, I never leave it to chance, hoping it will form itself. I have found it best to gain the insights from my leaders on what we can become in the future – the level of greatness we can achieve.

Our combined thoughts allow the raw clay of hope and excitement to be molded into a clear and inspiring work of *art*; a vision that embodies our desires for new and exciting results, while providing deeper levels of purpose. Visionary leaders transform their glimpses of hope into the big picture of their organizations.

Leadership Link Having vision is clearly seeing the mental image of what does not yet exist.

Share Vision

Having vision is critical, but if you are the only one who "sees" it, it does little good. Visionary leaders never keep their big picture a secret. They share it passionately, electrifyingly, and often. Clearly articulated as your Vision Statement, we must do more than merely post it on a website or on a wall. We must enthusiastically talk about it. Our vision provides everyone with the motivation and inspiration to keep going, even through the insurmountable obstacles and challenging circumstances on our path.

Visionary leaders do not solely own the vision. Instead, they share it as "Our" vision, not "My" vision. Vision can be shared in meetings, sent out in e-mails, discussed in departments, or talked about in one-on-one settings. But the best way to have it shared is to encourage all leaders to talk about it, and most importantly, to believe it and live it. The best vision is the one shared, so everyone can be empowered by "seeing" it.

Leadership Link Sharing vision is the physical step of enhancing belief levels so others can visualize your vision.

Stretch Vision

Sharing vision is essential, but it is detrimental to an organization if people know the vision, but it never materializes. Visionary leaders never allow vision to remain static. Instead they continue to stretch it and grow it, so they can move to it. Because vision is not yet realized, it is imperative that we inspire our team to take the necessary steps toward the horizon.

Stretching vision causes action, coupled with a sense of urgency. It drives behaviors and moves us in the right direction as we accomplish the objectives and goals required to consistently grow the glimpse of hope we originally began with. When we stretch vision, we open it up to discover ways to achieve it, establishing the boundaries we must cross and the comfort zones we must break through.

Leadership Link Stretching vision is the transformational process of achieving victories on the pathway to greater success.

While we can have vision and share vision, it is nearly impossible to stretch our own vision. It is only with the combined passion, compelling observations, and innovative ideas from our fellow leaders that we can consistently build upon, and expand, the initial flickers of a brighter and better future that first entered our minds.

With so much possible, we cannot afford to place vision on the backburner. It must be at the forefront of our thoughts and actions, and we need to consistently and energetically emphasize its importance, rallying our people to achieve it. To lead at this level, let's explore the environment required to support visionary leadership.

ECOSYSTEM FOR GREAT LEVELS OF GROWTH

If I gave you an object smaller than a marble, and asked you to place it in the ground, do you believe it could grow to over 350 feet high, 26 feet wide, and weigh more than one-million pounds? Does that even seem possible? Can something so small achieve such great levels of growth? Under the right conditions, it can and does happen naturally.

About fifty miles inland, along the coast of central California to southern Oregon, the seed of the Coastal Redwood grows and matures into trees that stretch far into the sky and can live for two-thousand years. For these trees, the environment is paramount for their growth and survival. They rely on the heavy fog of these areas as protection from the sun and drought. Although each tree can produce 100,000 seeds annually, very few take root.

Vision is similar. Multitudes of leaders have momentary thoughts of greatness, but most never take root. While not every redwood seed will rise to its true potential, those closest to the base of other trees stand a greater chance for survival. Vision stands the best chance for survival when it is the base of every visionary leader – the foundation of their dialogue and their actions.

Just as every aspect of their environment plays a critical role in the natural development of these behemoth trees, great vision requires a truly dynamic environment to grow. Leaders must pay attention to the conditions they allow in their organizations. Committed to achieving higher level results, visionary leadership is not designed to be a lonely position. We must foster an ecosystem that supports our vision and transforms more of our people into visionary leaders.

Leadership Link Schedule time into your day to share and discuss vision (vision statement).

VISIONARY ECOSYSTEM

Just as we focus on creating a unifying culture (Chapter 2) to enhance perceptions and provide an environment for leaders to flourish, we must provide the proper environment for our vision to flourish. Much like building a greenhouse for plants that require regulated climate conditions to grow, we must also create an ecosystem to support the development of our visionary leaders and the expansion (stretching) of our vision.

Like all environments on our planet, when the conditions are right, unprecedented levels of growth occur. Creating a visionary ecosystem will allow every leader, and potential leader, to understand the conditions necessary to support the vision at the highest levels. Visionary leadership is grown in a highly collaborative environment of mutual trust and respect.

I did not merely create a visionary ecosystem to support the achievement of 300 percent annual revenue growth, I protected and nurtured that environment, our greenhouse, because it provided the conditions necessary to build leaders who did more than support our plan. They had vision, shared vision, and stretched vision, with me. To become a leader at this level, let's explore what defines this exclusive role.

Leadership Link Transform your culture into a visionary ecosystem because vision can quickly fade away in a negative environment.

BRING THE HORIZON TO YOU

I have had the privilege of conducting thousands of leadership keynotes, workshops, and seminars across the country. In every session, I ask a simple question of my audience, "What do you expect from a leader?" As you can imagine, traits like integrity, empathy, and loyalty are quickly shared. But so is one other. Every industry, from the medical field to real estate, from the military to charity organizations, from banking to retail, confidently say the same thing, "Vision."

We know that they are not implying that they prefer to follow leaders who have better eyesight. No, they want to embark on a journey with a leader who has a vision for the future – a vision for *their* future. But when we fail to develop this ability in our leaders, we do more than miss out on the vast opportunities ahead of us, we dramatically let our team members down.

Some organizations, to their credit, have a vision statement, but most of their team members could not tell you what it is and most of their leaders struggle to recite even a portion of it. A vision statement, without the visionary leaders to carry it out, merely becomes a collection of well-crafted words. People not only need visionary leaders, they expect to have them.

While most leaders do not know what to do with the vision of their company, visionary leaders do not have that problem. They are literally moved by the vision and ensure that it is permeated throughout the entire team, manifesting into the productive actions required to achieve it. Visionary leaders do more than "see" all the incredible dreams on the horizon, they build a team of visionary leaders who bring the horizon to them.

Leadership Link Raise the bar on fostering visionary leadership.

The transition to visionary leadership is a great responsibility. It is both intimidating and exhilarating at the same time. Deciding to become a leader who has vision, shares it, and stretches it will not only forge you as a leader, it will significantly impact your entire team. To make the final link to becoming a visionary leader and transform the big picture of your organization into reality, focus on the three elite actions that will allow you to become the catalyst for positive enhancements.

These actions will do more than support the achievement of your vision, they will cultivate the leadership seeds required to grow other visionary leaders.

3 Elite Actions of a Visionary Leader:

1. Speak It

2. Fail Forward

3. Add Significance

Speak It

Most leaders are so overwhelmed with the present they rarely take the time to explore the unknown possibilities of the future, let alone talk about them. Regularly speaking about the future keeps things in perspective - what you are doing and why you are doing it. Most importantly, visionary leaders discuss *who* will be impacted as the vision is achieved.

Regardless of what is going on in their current world of challenges, issues, and hardships, speaking about the future allows leaders to keep their team members' thoughts focused on the positive aspects ahead of them instead of the difficulties in front of them. To enhance your visionary dialogue, use three key techniques.

1. Engage others in discussions about the results of the future

2. Strategize the actions required to attain them

3. Provide a clearer picture of the pathway to get there

Focusing on the future is not about ignoring the present. It is about allowing your team to visualize the completion of the vision, well in advance, which makes them feel more connected to it – and you. People who follow a visionary leader, feel like they are part of something special and great. Visionary leaders constantly open up dialogue about the future and what it will be like when they arrive at the destination.

Sometimes, we may face insurmountable odds, almost convincingly blocking the pathway to our vision. To keep his people focused on the vision, not the violence they faced, Gandhi spoke about the future when he told them, "When I despair, I remember that all through history the way truth and love have always won. There have been tyrants and murderers, and for a time, they can seem invincible, but in the end, they always fall. Think of it – always."

"In the end..." was his way of letting his people know that they will be victorious in the future.

Leadership Link Speaking about the future reiterates to your team that they are following a leader who is going somewhere.

Fail Forward

Visionary leaders may shine the light on the pathway to greatness, but it does not mean that every step taken is perfect. Fortunately, we are striving for progress, not perfection. But mistakes may happen along the journey, so it is imperative to encourage our people to fail forward.

Failing and leadership should never be spoken in the same sentence, right? Success might very well be the opposite of failure, but it is impossible to achieve extraordinary results without the valuable lessons learned through the experiences of failure. Vision can only be transformed into reality when actions are taken. But too many leaders are hesitant to move forward due to the fear of failing. Understandably so, some failures might cost them their job.

But visionary leaders create a balance in their ecosystem, removing fear from their leaders by creating an environment where unintentional failures are perceived as opportunities to self-improve; opportunities to discover new ways to exceed possibilities. It is never perfect when trying to transform dreams into reality, so strive for progress each day.

Visionary leadership is not achieved by getting everything right, but rather discovering ways of not doing it wrong. By stretching the vision of your leaders, they will transform failures into opportunities for growth, and will be empowered to take the risks necessary for unparalleled results. To properly allow your people to fail forward, use three key techniques.

1. Set acceptable levels of failure (boundaries)

2. Build higher levels of trust

3. Transform failures into opportunities to grow

Sometimes, we may stumble and fall on the pathway to our vision. To keep from giving up after each failure and defeat, Abraham Lincoln stayed focused on his vision and continued to *fail forward*.

- 1831 – Lost his job
- 1832 – Defeated for state Legislature
- 1833 – Failed in business
- 1836 – Suffered a nervous breakdown
- 1838 – Defeated for Illinois State Speaker
- 1843 – Defeated in run for Congress
- 1848 – Defeated again in run for Congress
- 1854 – Defeated in run for U.S. Senate
- 1856 – Defeated for Vice President
- 1858 – Defeated again in run for U.S. Senate
- **1960 – Elected the 16th President of the United Sates**

Fortunately, visionary leaders like Lincoln do not give up. For twenty-nine years, he continued to move forward, from failure to failure, learning from each experience. In 1963, Proclamation 95, also known as The Emancipation Proclamation, was issued by President Lincoln. This executive order impacted the lives of more than 3.5 million enslaved African Americans in the designated areas of the South by changing their federal legal status – from slaves to free people. Just two years later, he was assassinated.

Never give up on your vision. Visionary leaders are optimistic, seeing an opportunity in everything that occurs in their ecosystem. They look for areas of growth in every situation, and especially in every failure. They convey an understanding among all leaders that failing is only considered a failure when it stops someone from trying again.

All great leaders have suffered failures and visionary leaders teach their people how to seek the valuable lessons contained in every issue, problem, or setback. Never experience mere "failures." Instead, allow them to be "transformational learning experiences." Every failure can improve skills and increase confidence.

Leadership Link Failing forward provides the risk-takers in an environment to consistently move forward and not be held back by their failures.

Adding Significance

Leading an organization can often be a nearly thankless job, especially for leaders who fail to connect with people on a deeper level than merely job performance. I believe that the single greatest contribution we make, on our pathway to our vision, is to add significance to peoples' lives. Visionary leaders make an impact in who they are, not just what they do.

When leaders grow in an environment that adds significance to their lives, they stop criticizing and finger-pointing when things go wrong. They begin to work with others to seek out solutions. As those solutions are discovered, visionary leaders refuse credit, giving it to others and adding significance to their lives. Because adding significance is so significant, let's look at how to define it.

significance

noun

- The quality of being worthy.
- Being important.
- The meaning of someone or something.

If the greatest attributes of becoming a visionary leader is merely developing new products and services, expanding into new markets, or simply making more money, then we miss our greatest potential. We miss out on how to truly exceed possibilities when we fail to make people feel worthy, important, and like they have meaning.

Visionary leaders inspire other leaders because they are inspired themselves. By sharing the possibilities of creating an exciting future for their organization, visionary leaders encourage people to look for the exciting enhancements that await them in their personal and professional lives.

Visionary leaders teach others to view themselves as *victors* over their challenges, rather than being *victims* of their circumstances. This is a significant perception anyone can apply to their personal lives, not just their professional ones. Even if someone has been victimized, it is the perception of being a victim that will hold them back, keeping them from achieving even their own vision of a greater life. To consistently add significance to the lives of those you encounter, use three key techniques.

- Encourage people to improve
- Create solutions for their issues
- Give credit to others for their achievements

When Mother Teresa first saw her vision for the future, she described it as, "The call within the call." Her big picture was, "To leave the convent and help the poor while living among them." She dedicated her life to the poor, feeding them, dressing them, and taking care of them when they were sick. These were the people that others turned away from and merely walked by.

When others ignored them, she made them feel significant – she made them feel worthy, important, and let them know they had meaning. On the pathway to her vision, she said, "We think sometimes that poverty is only being hungry, naked and homeless. The poverty of being unwanted, unloved and uncared for is the greatest poverty. We must start in our own homes to remedy this kind of poverty."

Mother Teresa was keenly aware of her *Who* – the people who meant the most to her. She knew them by name and deeply cared about them. Standing only five feet tall, she was unstoppable on her quest to achieve her vision. Her true power came in the form of adding significance to the lives of others and she helped millions of people during her lifetime. Her good work continues in her name today.

Leadership
Link Adding significance ensures that visionary leaders never lose sight that everything we are doing is for the good of our people.

Visionary leaders are not recognized by the job they did; they are remembered by the impact they made. Gandhi, Martin Luther King Jr. and Mother Teresa are not known for their job skills. They are etched into history for their people skills.

Mohandas Karamchand Gandhi had a job. He was a lawyer. But he is known for the impact he made as the leader of the India independence movement.

Martin Luther King Jr. had a job. He was a Baptist minister. But he is known for the impact he made as the most visible leader and spokesperson in the civil rights movement.

Mother Teresa had a job. She was a Roman Catholic Nun. But she is known for the impact she made as the leader and founder of Missionaries for Charity.

What do you want to be known for?

UNLIMITED VISION

Leaders are only limited by their own vision, or more specifically, the lack of it. Creating an ecosystem that adds significance allows you to transform vision into reality. Vision is never achieved by chance, nor is it the side effect of merely being a good leader. It is the result of becoming a visionary leader who provides people with a new perspective for a bright future.

In the quest for greater results, most leaders attempt to differentiate their organization from the competition, through their products and services. While there is merit to this strategy, visionary leaders take a different approach, striving to differentiate their leaders from the leaders of their competitors. Having vision, sharing vision, and stretching vision should be a key duty in your job description...

- Responsible for consistently having vision, sharing vison, and stretching vision at the highest levels of excellence and enthusiasm.

Imagine if this was one of the duties in every leader's job description. As a visionary leader, we are the catalyst for a dynamic paradigm shift – one that will create a new and exciting destination. To arrive there, develop a team of leaders – a cohesive unit of visionary leaders. You have the ability to create an environment that improves performance, increases results, and impacts the lives of everyone who comes into contact with this new wave of leadership.

We have a Vision Statement at Think GREAT that guides us each day and provides us with a positive and an exciting look into the future. We discuss it at meetings and use it to make sure we are heading in the right direction.

Think GREAT Vision Statement:

Focused on creating a worldwide people movement, Think GREAT will be the international leader in personal and professional growth by increasing business elevation, developing high levels of engagement, and forging dynamic leaders.

In addition to our corporate Vision Statement, I also created a *Personal Vision Statement*, which further guides my actions and provides me with the greatest levels of clarity in my life. I encourage every leader to create their own Personal Vision Statement to provide a deeper level to your purpose. Mine is based on what I find the greatest value in... what I would do for free.

My Personal Vision Statement:

To enrich the lives of military families in a world free of cancer.

Short and sweet, I would do anything to achieve this vision. As a veteran, I have a sincere and genuine passion for our service members, veterans, and their families. Enriching their lives is a high priority to me. Because my wife is a four-time cancer survivor, I would do anything to help find a cure, so our daughter never has to hear the words, "You have cancer."

Once you have articulated your Personal Vision Statement, share it with team members, clients, prospects, and anyone you encounter. Give them a chance to know *who* you are, on a deeper level than your job description.

THE STEPS TOWARD LEADERSHIP

Every recruit begins their journey in the Marine Corps on the same yellow footprints. Our DI's never intended for us to remain motionless on them. We had to exhibit the courage to not only step forward but to keep going, despite all the challenges they had in store for us. The title of U.S. Marine is never handed out – we had to earn it.

Every leader has their own "yellow footprints" to step off and we take that bold move as we *make the decision to lead*. In most businesses, leaders want to learn the *art* of leading and guiding their teams on an expedition of discovery, growth, and success. The title of leader should never be handed out – we need to earn it.

But you now possess the guidebook, the manual, the premiere reference for consistently sharpening your leadership blade. *The Elite Leadership System (ELS)* provides the strategies and techniques necessary to fulfill your elite leadership purposes as you significantly improve your entire organization.

The ELS Expedition, shown on the next page, details *The Steps of Elite Leadership* required to transform yourself and your people into dynamic leaders who make an impact, not just in their businesses, but in the lives of everyone they encounter.

Dedicating yourself to becoming a better leader is one of the greatest decisions you will ever make. You will face challenges, but your resolve will continue to grow with each step you take, while simultaneously making a stronger connection between you and each of your people.

Be the leader who makes The LEADERSHIP Connection!

THE **ELS** EXPEDITION ™
The STEPS of ELITE LEADERSHIP

ELS
ELITE LEADERSHIP SYSTEM

STEP 1	STEP 2	STEP 3	STEP 4
ENHANCE PERCEPTIONS	ELEVATE PRIORITIES	EMPOWER PEOPLE	EXCEED POSSIBILITIES

Define Leadership	IN's & ON's	Dynamic Communication	Creating a Plan
Establish Identity	Rule of Thirds	Developing People	Building Leaders
Identify Goals	Accountability Tools	Think Tanks	Achieving Vision

Expedition Assessment

Leadership Performance Checklist

LEADERSHIP STEPS

BECOME A VISIONARY LEADER

Elite Leadership Step – Live Your Vision Statement

- Identify and enhance your Vision Statement – where you are going as an organization. With your leaders, ask each to share their personal meaning of the vision and how they believe it can be achieved.

  Next, encourage each leader to begin sharing the vision more often - in their meetings, with clients, and in their correspondence.

Additional Steps

- **Improvements:** Identify the areas that you need to improve as a Visionary Leader. Do you need to have more vision? Do you need to share it with greater passion? Are you ensuring that your vison and the vision of your leaders is consistently stretched?

- **Significance:** Make a list of the people in your personal and professional life that you want to make feel more significant. Sharpen your visionary leadership blade by making people feel worthy, important, special, and like they have great meaning.

- **Personal:** Beyond the scope of your corporate Vision Statement, compose a Personal Vision Statement – where are you going? What greater impact do you want to make in your family, your community, or in the world? Share your Personal Vision Statement so people understand *Who* you are and what you are unwavering *ON*.

Acknowledgments

My Deepest Gratitude

To my wife, Gina. Your constant support has not only encouraged me to complete this book but has inspired me to become a better leader. Thanks for supporting me.

To my son, Brandyn. Your artistic skills created the amazing "links" which grace the inside of this book. Thanks for bringing this book to life.

To my son, Jacob. Your personal commitment has always been a motivating force in my life. Thanks for always taking initiative.

To my daughter, Erika. Your hard work at my office helped me to stay on track with this book. Thanks for always holding me accountable.

About the Author

Erik Therwanger

Erik Therwanger began his unique career by serving in the U.S. Marine Corps as an air traffic controller. Leadership, honor, and integrity did not end after his four-year tour of duty; they became the foundation of his life, both personally and professionally.

After receiving the news that his wife had been diagnosed with cancer, Erik left his job in the entertainment industry, became her caregiver and started his new career in sales.

With no formal training, he began selling financial services. Relying on the strategies and techniques he learned as a Marine, he quickly became a top producer, recruiter, and trainer.

Erik returned to the entertainment industry and became the vice president of a media company in Santa Monica, CA. By building leaders, designing their strategic plan, and creating a dynamic sales system, he helped to raise annual sales by over 300%.

Erik's passion for helping others led to the creation of Think GREAT®. He successfully blends his leadership skills, his unparalleled ability to inspire and develop teams, and his wide array of strategic planning and sales experience, to provide practical solutions for individuals and organizations.

The Three Pillars of Business GREATNESS™ brings together the concepts from *The LEADERSHIP Connection, ELEVATE,* and *Dynamic Sales Combustion* to provide business leaders, and their teams, with a shared language of *leading, planning,* and *selling.*

Sharing his personal story and elite strategies, Erik's keynote speeches inspires audiences to strive for new levels of greatness. His interactive and powerful workshops highlight his step–by–step process for increasing results.

Erik delivers a compelling message that leaves a lasting impact in organizations, creating the necessary momentum to develop strong leaders, build visionary teams, and elevate sales results.

As the author of the Think GREAT® Collection, Erik has combined his challenging life experiences with his goal–setting techniques, to provide proven strategies to enhance the lives of others.

As a trainer and speaker for the spouses of armed services personnel, Erik is deeply aware of their challenges and sacrifices. To help support their education goals, Erik founded the *Think GREAT Foundation,* which is dedicated to awarding scholarships to the MilSpouse community. For more information, please visit:

www.ThinkGreatFoundation.org

ThinkGREAT®

www.ThinkGreat90.com

Please visit our website for more GREAT tools:

- Erik Therwanger's Keynote Speeches

- Workshops and Seminars

- Online Training Tools and Videos

- Register for the FREE Great Thought of the Week

More life-changing books in

- ELEVATE

- Dynamic Sales Combustion

- The GOAL Formula

- The SCALE Factor

- GPS: Goal Planning Strategy

- The Seeds of Success for LEADING

- The Seeds of Success for PLANNING

- The Seeds of Success for SELLING

Printed in the United States
By Bookmasters